The Genius of

American Education

THE GENIUS

OF AMERICAN

EDUCATION

❖❖❖❖❖❖❖❖❖❖❖❖❖❖❖❖❖❖❖❖❖❖❖❖❖❖❖❖❖❖

BY

Lawrence A. Cremin

Vintage Books

A DIVISION OF RANDOM HOUSE

New York

VINTAGE BOOKS

are published by

Alfred A. Knopf, Inc., and Random House, Inc.

Preface

THE THESIS of this volume is that the genius of American education—its animating spirit, its most distinctive quality—lies in the commitment to popularization. The three essays explore the bearing of this commitment on the structure, the nature, and the politics of present-day education. I see the analysis as basically an extension of the work I undertook in *The Transformation of the School* (1961), though my central effort here is didactic rather than historical, namely, to formulate a new, tough-minded progressivism that is at the same time consonant with the best in our tradition and appropriate to contemporary needs.

The essays were originally prepared under

the Horace Mann Lectureship at the University of Pittsburgh, the purpose of which is, in the words of the founders, to reaffirm Mann's faith in free schools and "to call to their service all citizens of this generation." It is a pleasure to record here my sense of honor at having been chosen Horace Mann Lecturer for 1965, and my appreciation for the hospitality extended me by Dean Paul Masoner, Professor Maurice Thomas, and their colleagues during my brief stay at the University. The essays were written during a year in residence at the Center for Advanced Study in the Behavioral Sciences, whose trustees and staff I should like to thank for many kindnesses, especially for providing the freedom and peace to think. And finally, the essays were edited by my associate, Judy F. Suratt, whose queries and suggestions, as always, went to the heart of the matter.

LAWRENCE A. CREMIN
Stanford, California
1965

Contents

The Genius of

American Education

I

⟨⟨⟨

The Commitment

to Popular Education

⟨⟨⟨

WE TEND TO THINK of popular education as a relatively recent phenomenon in the history of the West, associating it with the sweeping seventeenth- and eighteenth-century revolutions that ushered in the modern world.[1] Actually, the idea itself is much older, dating, as

[1] Parts of "The Commitment to Popular Education" were first presented in an address at the Harvard Graduate School of Education on July 16, 1964, and were subsequently published in the *Harvard Graduate School of Education Association Bulletin*, IX (Fall, 1964), 2-6.

it does, from the earliest systematic specula-
tions on the nature of human polity. The
classic treatise, of course, is Plato's *Republic*,
which remains to this day the most penetrat-
ing analysis of education and politics ever un-
dertaken. Recall Plato's argument: In order
to talk about the good life, we have to talk
about the good society; and in order to talk
about the good society, we have to talk about
the kind of education that will bring that society into existence and sustain it. Hence,
there is no vision of the good life that does not
imply a set of educational policies; and con-
versely, every educational policy has implicit
in it a vision of the good life.

Recall, too, that when Plato gets around to
talking about education, he gives relatively
little attention to schools. As far as Plato is
concerned, it is the community that educates,
by which he means all the influences that
mold the mind and character of the young:
music, architecture, drama, painting, poetry,
laws, and athletics. It is this insight, of course,
that leads him ultimately to his outrageous but
nonetheless profound suggestion that if you
want to build and sustain the good society,
you have to choose the wisest men and give

4

them complete power over all the agencies that educate. Hence, his proposal for the rule of society by philosopher-kings, who were, I suppose, to be our first professional education-ists.

Alfred North Whitehead once quipped that all of Western philosophy has been a series of footnotes to Plato, and certainly in education this has been the case. Every major philosopher since Plato has written on education, and every one of them has been governed in some way or other by Plato's insights. And similarly, every major political system from Athens on has had to see to the training of the young for the perpetuation of the values it holds most dear.

In our own country, it was Thomas Jefferson who first articulated the inextricable tie between education and the politics of a free society. "If a nation expects to be ignorant and free," he wrote, "in a state of civilization, it expects what never was and never will be." [2] We are all familiar with the proposal he made to the Virginia legislature for a state educa-

[2] Thomas Jefferson to Colonel Charles Yancey, January 6, 1816, in Paul Leicester Ford, ed., *The Writings of Thomas Jefferson* (10 vols.; New York: G. P. Putnam's Sons, 1892-99), X, 4.

tion system that would offer three years of public schooling to every free white child of the Commonwealth and then send the brightest youngsters on to grammar school and college free of charge. Jefferson's plan was turned down, but one can trace an unbroken line of influence from Jefferson to Horace Mann to John Dewey—and to trace it to Dewey is, like it or not, to trace it to ourselves.

There is a subtle shift of emphasis when the idea gets to Dewey, however, that is worth discussing, since it highlights certain crucial elements in the American theory of popular education. Jefferson was a great believer in schooling, but it never occurred to him that schooling would be the chief educational influence on the young. Schooling might provide technical skills and basic knowledge, but it was the press and participation in politics that really educated the citizenry. Public education was to be only one part of the education of the public, and a relatively minor part at that. The same was true for Horace Mann's generation, which built our modern state public school systems but which also organized public libraries and lyceums, founded mechanics' institutes and agricultural societies, invented penny newspapers and dime novels, and created the popular political parties we know today. To be sure, Mann's own special crusade was for common schools, which he believed held the key to all human progress. But his contemporaries were far less single-minded in their efforts at popular enlightenment. Consider, for example, James De Bow's exhortation to his countrymen in 1854: "Let us diffuse knowledge throughout the length and breadth of this great country; multiply the means of information,—send the schoolmaster into every hovel,—dot every hill with the schoolhouse and college,—let the Press, without intermission, night and day, pour forth its steady streams of light,—foster Science and the Arts,—let the civilizing and godlike influences of machinery uninterruptedly extend. Then will the future of our country open, boundless and great, beyond all example, beyond all compare, and countless ages bless its mission and acknowledge its glorious dominion." [3] However high-flown the rhetoric, there is no mistaking the diversity of approach to the problem of educating the public. When it

[3] *De Bow's Review*, XVII (New Series, IV) (1854), 123.

came to education, De Bow wanted more of it, in all its forms.

Dewey's generation may have started out with the same insights, but it transformed them fundamentally. We can see the transformation in the pages of *Democracy and Education,* undoubtedly the most significant work on popular education written in the twentieth century. Dewey begins by assuring us that all of life educates and that deliberate education represents only one small part of the total education of the child. Furthermore, he tells us, there are many forms of deliberate education, including that given by the home, the shop, the neighborhood, and the school. So far, Dewey is a Platonist. But then he advances the characteristic complaint of early twentieth-century progressives: industrialism is destroying the traditional home, shop, neighborhood, and church; they are no longer performing their educational functions; some other institution must take on these functions; *ergo*—and here, Dewey takes the *grand jeté* of twentieth-century educational theory—the school must do so. By the middle of the book, Dewey is talking about the public school as society's great instrument for shaping its own destiny. Public education has become coextensive with the education of the public.

Now, Dewey knew full well that schooling is at best but one method for molding the young, and in some respects a superficial method at that. Moreover, he shared with his contemporaries a sense of the power and influence of other forms of education. Indeed, in his continuing dialogue with Walter Lippmann during the 1920's, he pointed again and again to the decisive role of the press in developing an enlightened public opinion. But it was to the school that he always returned, as the institution best organized to serve democracy's cause. His decision was a fateful one for American educational theory; for while it doubtless infused popular schooling with new vitality and high purpose, it effectively removed the agencies of informal education from the purview of public educators. With the extraordinary development of these agencies in succeeding years, the education of the public would pass slowly but inexorably into other, less responsible hands. Dewey could hardly have anticipated these developments; yet even his later work never fully took account of them. And for years his disciples continued to confuse notions of schooling "the whole child" with nonsense about providing the child's whole education.

Be that as it may, a newly self-conscious teaching profession quickly took up Dewey's formulations; and more importantly, so did the lay public. To study the literature of the Progressive era is to be overwhelmed by the extent to which political reform is conceived essentially in educational terms. Negroes sought to achieve equality of citizenship by gaining access to popular schooling. Farmers and workingmen attempted to retain their share of the national income by promoting programs of vocational education. Humanitarians attacked the problem of poverty by establishing curricula in civics, hygiene, and domestic science. And businessmen reached for industrial supremacy by extending the scope of technical training. The result of these efforts was a radical redefinition of the school, one that plunged it squarely into the struggle for a better life.[4]

That redefinition has been under sharp at-

[4] I deal with the redefinition at length in *The Transformation of the School: Progressivism in American Education, 1876-1957* (New York: Alfred A. Knopf, 1961).

tack in recent years, but for all intents and purposes it remains contemporary. Eight years ago, when the Russians beat us into space, the public blamed the schools, not realizing that the only thing that had been proved, as the quip went at the time, was that their German scientists had gotten ahead of our German scientists. And today, almost a decade after Sputnik, the most rapidly growing area of the secondary school curriculum is not physics, not chemistry, not mathematics, but driver education. Hear the argument: Fifty thousand people a year are being killed on the highways; obviously, traditional forms of driving instruction are not working; some new institution must assume the responsibility; the school must do it. It is a curious solution, requiring courses instead of seat belts, but typically American. One of my friends likes to remark that in other countries, when there is a profound social problem there is an uprising; in the United States, we organize a course!

2

Dewey published *Democracy and Education* in 1916, and we are still governed by its precepts. Yet an educational revolution was in the making at the very time *Democracy and Education* appeared, that was destined to outmode certain of its formulations. I refer to the rapid development of the mass media of communication, of private and quasi-public youth groups of every sort and variety, and of formal educational programs outside the aegis of public school authorities. The number of daily newspapers reached a peak in 1914—almost 2,500—and although that number has declined, circulation figures have risen steadily. D. W. Griffith produced *The Birth of a Nation* in 1915, introducing many of the techniques we have come to associate with the modern cinema. Commercial radio began in 1920 with the first regular broadcasts of station KDKA in Pittsburgh. And, as we all know, commercial television began in earnest right after World War II. Today, there are 1,843 daily newspapers, almost 9,000 weekly newspapers, over 650 television stations, some 3,860 AM and 1,340 FM radio stations, several hundred book publishers, who in 1964 issued over 28,000 titles, literally scores of movie producers, who in 1963 issued almost 10,000 films, and, as Wilbur Schramm once remarked, so many magazines of so many kinds that one never knows quite how to define a magazine, and it is therefore difficult to say whether there are 7,500 or 10,000 of them.[5]

As for youth groups, even before World War 1 millions of youngsters took part in the activities of the YMCA, the YWCA, the Boy Scouts, the Girl Scouts, and the Camp Fire Girls. These enterprises burgeoned during the 1930's, when the United Christian Youth Movement probably reached over ten million young people all over the world. Today, there are countless youth organizations of a local, national, and international character.

And as for formal educational programs not under public school sponsorship, we are only beginning to realize their scope and power.

[5] The statistics are taken from *The World Almanac* for 1965, *N. W. Ayer & Son's Directory of Newspapers and Periodicals, 1965*, the *International Motion Picture Almanac* for 1965, and *Publishers' Weekly*, CLXXXVII (January 18, 1965).

Harold Clark and Harold Sloan have been studying such efforts over the past eight years and have come up with some extraordinary findings, among them, that more advanced instruction in mathematics and the natural sciences is given by companies such as General Electric or Bell Telephone than by any American university; that the armed forces are far ahead of the schools in the productive use of instructional technology; and that in many communities, more money is being spent on formal instruction outside the schools than on instruction within.[6]

My point is that all these agencies educate the public, and no serious discussion of contemporary educational policy can afford to ignore them. I am not arguing that schools are uninfluential or that all this education is of equal worth. I am simply urging that those who call themselves educators bear in mind the total education of the public and the many agencies that carry it on.

[6] Harold F. Clark and Harold S. Sloan, *Classrooms in the Factories* (Rutherford, N.J.: Institute of Research, Fairleigh Dickinson University, 1958); *Classrooms in the Stores* (Sweet Springs, Mo.: Roxbury Press, 1962); and *Classrooms in the Military* (New York: Bureau of Publications, Teachers College, Columbia University, 1964).

Strangely enough, it is the dictators of our time who have understood most fully the revolutionary implications of what my colleague Martin Dworkin has called "the new architecture of education." [7] Goebbels' diary, for example, records his first conversation with Hitler on the subject of a special propaganda ministry early in 1932. "The idea," Goebbels wrote, "was that of a Ministry for popular education, in which Cinema, Radio, new educational institutions, Art, Culture and Propaganda would be brought together under one administration. . . . It is an enormous project, which in its kind has never yet existed. I am already beginning to work out the plans for this Ministry. It is to serve the purpose of building the intellectual-spiritual foundation of our power and of capturing not only the

[7] The phrase itself recurs throughout Dworkin's lectures on "Education, Ideology, and Mass Communication" at Teachers College, Columbia University, and reflects a point of view that has been of signal influence in the development of these essays. See Dworkin's regular cinema criticism in the *Progressive* from 1952 to 1962, in which one continuing theme was the film as a form of popular education, and his editorial introductions to the several volumes in the Teachers College Press series, *Studies in Culture and Communication*, especially, the Earl of Listowel, *A Critical History of Modern Aesthetics;* A. V. Judges, ed., *The Function of Teaching;* and Lewis Jacobs, *The Rise of the American Film.*

apparatus of the state but the people as a whole." The Ministry was established by decree in March of 1933. The following September, the Nazis created a *Kulturkammer*, or Chamber of Culture, which brought together under the Ministry of Propaganda and Public Enlightenment the press, radio, the theater, literature, music, the plastic arts, and cinema. Needless to say, the schools and the Hitler Youth were closely coordinated with the Chamber.[8]

The Soviet Union followed much the same pattern during the latter years of Stalin's regime. Stalin is said to have remarked to H. G. Wells that education is a weapon, whose effect depends on who holds it in his hands and at whom it is aimed. Once in power, Stalin acted on this belief. The whole social and cultural apparatus of the state—youth groups, industrial unions, farmer cooperatives, professional organizations, schools, the press, radio, the theater, literature, music, science, even recreation—all were forged into the single mighty system of mind control described by

[8] Edward Yarnell Hartshorne, Jr., *The German Universities and National Socialism* (Cambridge, Mass.: Harvard University Press, 1937), pp. 29-31.

George S. Counts in *The Country of the Blind* (1949). True, the situation has changed somewhat since the death of Stalin, but Stalin's effort remains for all to contemplate. In a sense, the whole modern concept of totalitarianism is fundamentally an educational idea, made possible by the theory and technology of twentieth-century communication.

3

Of course, democracy too can be viewed as an educational idea, made possible by the theory and technology of twentieth-century communication. Recall Dewey's argument in *Democracy and Education.* "A democracy," he tells us, "is more than a form of government; it is primarily a form of associated living, of conjoint communicated experience. The extension in space of the number of individuals who participate in an interest so that each has to refer his own action to that of others, and to consider the action of others to give point and direction to his own, is equivalent to the breaking down of those barriers of class, race, and national territory which kept men from perceiving the full import of their activity. These more numerous and more varied points of contact denote a greater diversity of stimuli to which an individual has to respond; they consequently put a premium on variation in his action. They secure a liberation of powers which remain suppressed as long as the incitations to action are partial, as they must be in a group which in its exclusiveness shuts out many interests." [9]

This widening of shared concerns and this liberation of personal capacities, Dewey goes on to say, are not in the first place products of deliberate effort. They derive from the modes of commerce and communication we associate with industrialism. But once they have been set in motion, "it is a matter of deliberate effort to sustain and extend them." Thus, the need arises for a particular form of education that encourages the intellectual and moral individuality indispensable to social progress, and at the same time cultivates the power to

[9] John Dewey, *Democracy and Education* (New York: The Macmillan Co., 1916), p. 101.

join freely and fully in shared or common activities.

The key to this particular form of education lies in Dewey's conception of "growth," a term that has been much abused by his disciples and critics alike. Growth, he tells us, is "constant expansion of horizons and consequent formation of new purposes and new responses." [10] Therefore, when he argues that education is a continuous process of growth, having as its aim at every stage an added capacity for growth, he is merely saying that the aim of education is to make, not citizens or workers or soldiers or even scientists, but human beings who will live life to the fullest, who will never stop expanding their horizons, reformulating their purposes, and modifying their actions in light of these purposes.[11] Given this conception of growth, a democracy can be defined simply as a society in which each individual is encouraged to continue his education throughout his lifetime.[12]

[10] *Ibid.*, p. 206.
[11] *Ibid.*, pp. 60-2, 362.
[12] *Ibid.*, p. 117.

It is an admirable definition, I think, and one characteristically American in its humanity and optimism. And more importantly, perhaps, we hold in our hands for the first time in history the means of realizing just such a society. It is more than a matter of rising school and university enrollments, though these are certainly significant in their own right. It is rather a matter of a vastly increasing diversity of educational opportunities now open to anyone who would avail himself of them.

Some years ago, Margaret Mead, in a fascinating essay on obsolescence in our education system, drew a distinction between the *vertical* transmission of the tried and true from a mature teacher to an immature student and the *lateral* transmission of what has just been discovered or invented or created to every sentient member of society.[13] Schools by their very nature, she indicated, emphasize the vertical transmission of knowledge; and hence, in a world of rapid change, they are forever doomed to obsolescence. What is needed, she suggested, is a recasting of our traditional con-

[13] Margaret Mead, "Thinking Ahead: Why Is Education Obsolete?" *Harvard Business Review*, XXXVI (November-December, 1958), 23-30.

cepts in such a way that primary education would refer to that stage of education in which children are taught what they need to know in order to be fully human in the world in which they are growing up and secondary education would refer to whatever further education is obtained during the individual's whole lifetime. Obviously, primary education would embrace advanced as well as elementary studies in the sciences and humanities; while secondary education would include not only conventional types of schooling but also "types of work training not yet or only now being developed."

It was a remarkably prescient proposal, forecasting, as it did, the numerous manpower training programs inaugurated during the Kennedy and Johnson administrations. Even so, it did not go far enough in its effort at reformulation. For the fact is that children learn what they need to know to be fully human in the present world from a variety of institutions. They come to school believing and valuing a host of things the school never taught them, and they continue to learn from other agencies throughout their school years. To talk intelligently about primary education, even in the sense in which Miss Mead uses the phrase, we have to consider the total range of intellectual and moral influences that pervade the child's world, and then assess the school's particular responsibilities in light of that consideration. Once again, this is not to argue that the schools have no traditional or characteristic functions; it is merely to urge that we discuss those functions realistically in the context of the total educational situation.

David Riesman once advanced the intriguing suggestion that schools ought to exert a countervailing influence in our culture—that is, they ought to oppose the dramatic pendulum swings of public opinion that seem to occur from generation to generation.[14] His suggestion has a good deal of merit; after all, one definition of an intellectual is a man who thinks otherwise. But Riesman's ideal could easily become as inflexible as Dewey's concern for bringing the schools closer to life. In the last analysis, what the school is uniquely equipped to do, given the range of agencies that educate, is to make youngsters aware of

[14] David Riesman, *Constraint and Variety in American Education* (Lincoln, Neb.: University of Nebraska Press, 1956), pp. 23-30.

the constant bombardment of facts, opinions, and values to which they are subjected; to help them question what they see and hear; and, ultimately, to give them the intellectual resources they need to make judgments and assess significance.

In order to do this, however, teachers must develop far greater insight than they now possess into the work of other educative agencies. Permit me a few brief illustrations from the world of commercial television, anno Domini 1965. We have, for example, the interesting experience of the National Broadcasting Company with its Saturday morning program *Exploring*. Begun in the latter part of 1962, in the wake of Congressional investigations into the impact of television violence on youngsters, the program is a fascinating intellectual potpourri for children (though half of its 5.2 million viewers happen to be adults). Presided over by a genial physicist named Albert Hibbs, it will range on any given Saturday from music to history to the new mathematics; and it uses every conceivable pedagogical device to dramatize its presentations: puppets, models, and magicians; songs, stories, and cartoons. Not surprisingly, the program has elicited enormous enthusiasm from coast to coast. But what is of special interest is that more and more elementary schools are now devoting part of Friday's classwork to preparing for Saturday's television presentation, using a guide supplied gratis by NBC that now reaches more than half the elementary teachers of the country. Make no mistake: NBC is in the business of popular education (to say nothing of teacher education); and given its technical staff and production facilities, it can doubtless teach certain material more effectively and more economically than any school now in existence.

Exploring conveys information directly, and there is relatively little difficulty in estimating its influence. Consider, on the other hand, the far more complicated problem of the vocational models youngsters see on television. The point is commonly made that present-day children, unlike their grandparents, grow up in a world in which they rarely see people doing the jobs they themselves might aspire to do. As a result, job selection becomes a somewhat haphazard affair, which often has little to do with one's particular aptitudes and abilities. To be sure, vocational guidance grew up at the turn of the century precisely in an effort to introduce a modicum of rationality into the process; and today, the guidance counselor is an increasingly familiar figure on the high school scene. But the point is that youngsters are also getting a good deal of "guidance" from the subtle but immensely persuasive characterizations they see day in and day out on television—of physicians and nurses on *Dr. Kildare*, of journalists on *The Reporter*, of lawyers on *The Defenders*, of soldiers on *Combat*, of teachers on *Mr. Novak*, and of forest rangers on *Lassie*. They receive images of professional life—and, indeed, of life styles in general—that are often dramatically engrossing but only partially accurate.[15] Once again, the school's business is to systematize and criticize; and teachers can do this only if they recognize the enormous power of television in presenting interpretations of reality to their students.

Finally, we ought to consider Louis Harris' recent assertion in *Newsweek* that the current civil rights movement is preëminently a television revolution, inspired by the expectations

[15] See Harris Dienstfrey, "Doctors, Lawyers & Other TV Heroes," *Commentary*, XXXV (1963), 519-24.

Negro citizens have learned from television programs and commercials. Indeed, Harris believes that it is television more than any other educational agency that is bringing the Negro into the mainstream of American life. "There is a TV set in nine Negro homes out of ten," he wrote in 1963, "poking out an antenna that senses the white world and its ways as never before. In a world of hungering men, even a soap commercial can throw sparks of revolt if its setting is a modern suburban kitchen." [16] Add to this the systematic education of the public in the nature and urgency of the Negro revolution—through news broadcasts, public service programs, and Presidential addresses before joint sessions of Congress—and we begin to gain a sense of the unparalleled power of television as an agency for molding and influencing public opinion. [17]

Granted this, it should be added immediately that we have far too little solid empirical

[16] *Newsweek*, LXII (July 29, 1963), 16.
[17] See James Reston's incisive comments on Lyndon B. Johnson's Civil Rights Address of March 15, 1965 (which is estimated to have reached thirty-five million homes and seventy million persons) in the *New York Times*, March 17, 1965, p. 44.

knowledge of the actual processes by which individuals acquire their values, tastes, and commitments. The recent work of James Coleman and Nevitt Sanford has stressed the extraordinary influence of the peer culture, which often contradicts everything the school itself is trying to do.[18] And there is also Philip Jacob's intriguing summary of the research dealing with the impact of social science teaching on student attitudes, published under the title *Changing Values in College* (1957). Jacob found that in most colleges, the impact of formal teaching is virtually nil, that it is the students who exert the real influence. Only in a few institutions, where faculty and student values have somehow converged, do professors appear to have any appreciable effect.

The literature on the popular media is less conclusive. Investigators like Joseph T. Klapper or Paul Lazarsfeld or Robert Merton or Hilde T. Himmelweit can tell us how many individuals watched what programs for how many hours, how often they attended what

[18] James Coleman, *The Adolescent Society* (New York: The Free Press of Glencoe, 1961) and Nevitt Sanford, ed., *The American College* (New York: John Wiley & Sons, 1962).

movies, and how frequently they read what newspapers and magazines.[19] But when it comes to the real question of the influence of all this, there is sharp disagreement, running from the shrill warnings of Fredric Wertham that comic books and television are literally making delinquents of our youth, to the comforting rebuttals of his fellow psychiatrists who contend that comic books and television programs simply provide healthy catharses for youthful aggression. And beyond this, there is Wilbur Schramm's more general observation that today's schoolman is dealing with an audience that is receiving more communication than ever before, but of a kind that encourages acceptance rather than criticism, withdrawal rather than participation, fantasy rather than realism.[20]

The fact is we need a vast number of systematic scholarly studies of education in all

[19] See Wilbur Schramm, ed., *The Process and Effects of Mass Communication* (Urbana, Ill.: University of Illinois Press, 1954); Joseph T. Klapper, *The Effects of Mass Communication* (New York: The Free Press of Glencoe, 1960); and Lotte Bailyn, ed., "The Uses of Television," *Journal of Social Issues*, XVIII (1962), 1-61.
[20] Wilbur Schramm, "Mass Media and Educational Policy," in Nelson B. Henry, ed., *Social Forces Influencing American Education* (Chicago: University of Chicago Press, 1961), p. 209.

its forms, studies that will take us far beyond where we now are in comprehending the peculiar potency of institutions like the Bronx High School of Science and Swarthmore College; or in understanding why some youngsters yield to the depressing influences of slums while others transcend them; or, indeed, in grasping the almost magical persuasiveness of a television personality like Captain Kangaroo or a magazine like *Seventeen*. Only in the light of such studies shall we ever be able to talk authoritatively about popular education in its most comprehensive and significant sense.

4

In effect, what I have been trying to suggest is the host of new relationships and problems inherent in the educational revolution of our time. There is no doubt that this generation of American children will experience a range of formal and informal education unparalleled in history. They will spend their whole lives in and out of classrooms of one sort or another, though many of these will not be called classrooms. They will have access to facilities that are only now in the process of being developed: pre-school learning laboratories, children's art museums, community science centers, summer music camps, adult recreation centers, public television networks, vocational retraining programs, and regional research libraries. And they will enjoy in their homes to an unprecedented degree the wisdom, the art, and the experience of other ages and other peoples. This education will be provided by a multitude of agencies—public and private, national and local, religious and secular, military and civilian—and it will be supported by taxes, tithes, and tuition fees, by grants from foundations and gifts from corporations.

Why all this education? To what purpose? There are no more important questions for us to be asking, and yet we have asked them neither insistently nor well in recent years. Indeed, if anything, we seem deliberately to have turned away from them, in the spirit, perhaps, of James B. Conant's barb about the "sense of distasteful weariness" that overtakes him every time someone sets out to define education.[21] One can understand why, for much of the recent literature of educational philosophy has been drearily polemical or narrowly analytical, and seemingly of little relevance to the tasks at hand. But philosophical problems do not resolve themselves by being ignored, and it will do Americans little good to quicken their pace in education if they do not know where they are going.

It is here that I return to Dewey's definition of a democratic society. We are a pragmatic people, and we have justified our educational programs essentially in pragmatic terms. Education is good economics, sensible politics, and sound defense; it trains character, helps people get ahead, and incidentally keeps them off the labor market for protracted periods of time. All these arguments, of course, are quite valid: education does create wealth; it does heighten the desire for achievement; it does promote political stability; and it does enhance military

[21] James Bryant Conant, *The Child, the Parent, and the State* (Cambridge, Mass.: Harvard University Press, 1959), p. 1.

effectiveness.[22] But such justifications are only immediate in character. The ultimate justification of a democratic educational program must lie in its ability to enhance the quality of individual lives, or, to use Dewey's phraseology, to encourage the intellectual, moral, and aesthetic growth of individual human beings.

Now, the "growth" metaphor itself is not without its difficulties, as a number of perceptive critics have pointed out.[23] In Dewey's usage, it presupposed certain values and com-

[22] The recent work of the social scientists has been most valuable here. See, for example, Theodore W. Schultz, *The Economic Value of Education* (New York: Columbia University Press, 1963); Frederick Harbison and Charles A. Myers, *Education, Manpower, and Economic Growth* (New York: McGraw-Hill Book Co., 1964); Gary S. Becker, *Human Capital* (New York: National Bureau of Economic Research, 1964); David C. McClelland, *The Achieving Society* (Princeton, N.J.: D. Van Nostrand Co., 1961); and Gabriel A. Almond and Sidney Verba, *The Civic Culture* (Princeton, N.J.: Princeton University Press, 1963).

[23] See Max Black, *Models and Metaphors* (Ithaca, N.Y.: Cornell University Press, 1962), Chap. 3; Israel Scheffler, *The Language of Education* (Springfield, Ill.: Charles C. Thomas, 1960), pp. 47-59, and "Philosophical Models of Teaching," *Harvard Educational Review*, XXXV (1965), 131-43; and R. S. Peters, *Education as Initiation* (London: The University of London Institute of Education, 1964). Note Black's interesting conclusion: "No doubt metaphors are dangerous—and perhaps especially so in philosophy. But a prohibition against their use would be a willful and harmful restriction upon our powers of inquiry."

mitments of the larger society that would indicate the particular directions in which
growth should be encouraged; and it always
implied an increasing measure of rationality
in the ordinary business of living.[24] Without
such correlatives, the idea of growth is easily
perverted into a vague and romantic justification for practically anything, as the history of
the progressive education movement so well
demonstrates. It is in this light, it seems to me,
that John Gardner's book *Excellence* (1961)
takes on such significance. For it preserves the
equalitarianism implicit in the Deweyan idea
of growth—everyone, after all, is capable of
growth—and ties it to a conception of quality
sufficiently broad to meet the requirements of
a democratic-industrial civilization. "A conception which embraces many kinds of excellence at many levels," Gardner has written,
"is the only one which fully accords with the
richly varied potentialities of mankind; it is

[24] Dewey, *Democracy and Education*, Chap. 7, and
John L. Childs, *Education and Morals* (New York:
Appleton-Century-Crofts, 1950), Chap. 2. Growth also
implied systematic study of the academic disciplines,
which represent the refined wisdom of the race; see pp.
47-61 *infra*, particularly footnote 13, and John Dewey,
The Child and the Curriculum (Chicago: University of
Chicago Press, 1902).

the only one which will permit high morale throughout the society. . . . We need excellent physicists and excellent mechanics. We need excellent cabinet members and excellent first-grade teachers. The tone and fiber of our society depend upon a pervasive and almost universal striving for good performance." [25] Given such a view, growth could well be defined as the deliberate effort to achieve excellence in every domain of life.

What if we were to take the Deweyan idea of growth and apply it as a standard in assessing the agencies of popular education? What if we were to judge each institution and program by the extent to which it helps individuals expand their horizons, heighten their sensibilities, and rationalize their actions? The results would be radical indeed. In the formal education system, we might abandon utilitarian trivia in favor of those experiences that place a premium on learning how to learn, so that students could go on learning even after they had left the schools. [26] Outside the formal system, we might nurture those standards of

[25] John W. Gardner, *Excellence: Can We Be Equal and Excellent Too?* (New York: Harper & Brothers, 1961), pp. 131-32.

[26] Dewey, *Democracy and Education*, pp. 60-1.

taste and judgment that would lead the public to demand more numerous and extensive oases amidst the wastelands of commercial art and entertainment. And in the society at large, we might some day come to demand of all our institutions that they exert a continuing educative influence on individuals. It is such policies, I think, that are patently implied when we commit ourselves to the worth and dignity of every human being.

In the last analysis, there is no more humane view of education than as growth in understanding, sensibility, and character, and no more noble view of democracy than as the dedication of society to the lifelong education of all its members.

II

◇◇◇◇◇◇◇◇◇◇◇◇◇◇◇◇◇◇◇◇◇◇◇◇◇◇◇◇◇◇◇◇◇◇◇◇◇

Popular Education and

Popular Culture

◇◇◇◇◇◇◇◇◇◇◇◇◇◇◇◇◇◇◇◇◇◇◇◇◇◇◇◇◇◇◇◇◇◇◇◇◇

I AM ONE OF the many who have always found Thomas Jefferson contemporary. This is not to say that I agree with everything he ever said; that, as a matter of fact, would be especially difficult for an unregenerate admirer of those great cities Jefferson found so cancerous to the body politic. It is rather to say that I derive continuing inspiration from his work. Jefferson was one of those remarkable men who always seem to be talking about the right issues in the right way at the right time.

Certainly this is so with respect to his writings on education. Consider, as an instance, his discussion of the aims and purposes of a republican school system, which he included in his celebrated Rockfish Gap Report on the program of the University of Virginia. The objects of primary education, he noted, were:

To give to every citizen the information he needs for the transaction of his own business;

To enable him to calculate for himself, and to express and preserve his ideas, his contracts and accounts, in writing;

To improve, by reading, his morals and faculties;

To understand his duties to his neighbors and country, and to discharge with competence the functions confided to him by either;

To know his rights; to exercise with order and justice those he retains; to choose with discretion the fiduciary of those he delegates; and to notice their conduct with diligence, with candor, and judgment;

And, in general, to observe with intelligence and faithfulness all the social relations under which he shall be placed.

The objects of higher education, Jefferson went on to say, were:

To form the statesmen, legislators and judges, on whom public prosperity and individual happiness are so much to depend;

To expound the principles and structure of government, the laws which regulate the intercourse of nations, those formed municipally for our own government, and a sound spirit of legislation, which, banishing all arbitrary and unnecessary restraint on individual action, shall leave us free to do whatever does not violate the equal rights of another;

To harmonize and promote the interests of agriculture, manufactures and commerce, and by well informed views of political economy to give a free scope to the public industry;

To develop the reasoning faculties of our youth, enlarge their minds, cultivate their morals, and instill into them the precepts of virtue and order;

To enlighten them with mathematical and physical sciences, which advance the arts, and administer to the health, the subsistence, and comforts of human life;

And, generally, to form them to habits of reflection and correct action, rendering them examples of virtue to others, and of happiness within themselves.

Finally, the objects of grammar school education—the phrase "secondary education" would have been unfamiliar to Jefferson—were to serve some youths as the "passage of entrance" into the university, and to afford others "the means of being qualified for the various vocations of life, needing more instruction than merely menial or praedial labor." [1]

I have taken the liberty of quoting Jefferson at length, since it seems to me there is an extraordinary freshness and cogency about

[1] "Report of the Commissioners Appointed to Fix the Site of the University of Virginia, &c.," in Roy J. Honeywell, *The Educational Work of Thomas Jefferson* (Cambridge, Mass.: Harvard University Press, 1931), pp. 248-60.

his proposals. They expressly embrace the complementary commitments of a free society to equality and to excellence, guaranteeing a minimum of education to all citizens and offering further education to those who desire it and qualify. They bespeak a breadth of educational purpose rare in Jefferson's time or in any other: agriculture, manufacturing, and commerce; the sciences and the arts; the mundane and the spiritual—all will thrive under the beneficent influence of widespread learning. They recognize that true education forms individuals, who then and only then become "examples of virtue to others, and of happiness within themselves"; and they indicate the concomitant responsibility of education to promote the health and welfare of the commonwealth.

I suppose there is a sense in which we can portray the whole course of American educational history as the gradual realization of the Jeffersonian ideal; indeed, that is exactly what Conant has done in his intriguing little book *Thomas Jefferson and the Development of American Public Education* (1962). My interest at this point, however, is in the extent to which American educational debate over the past hundred and fifty years can be viewed as a series of arguments for one aspect of Jefferson's program as opposed to another: the practical *versus* the liberal; the individual *versus* the social; and most important, perhaps, the elitist *versus* the equalitarian. Jefferson's wisdom was that he saw the educational requirements of a free society whole and in balance; unfortunately, too few of his countrymen then or since have been as comprehensive or as equitable in their proposals for the schools.

Both Mann and Dewey, of course, were thoroughly steeped in the Jeffersonian tradition, though each in his own way sought to effect certain reformulations. Mann was an uncompromising equalitarian, who never tired of insisting—occasionally with appropriate allusions to Jefferson—that the general diffusion of knowledge rather than the liberal education of leaders should be the paramount concern of a republican society. "The scientific or literary well-being of a community," he liked to argue, "is to be estimated not so much by its possessing a few men of great knowledge, as its having many men of competent knowledge." [2] Hence, the priority of common schools in the development of public education systems. Mann's argument was no doubt an appealing one to Jacksonian Americans, though we should bear in mind that those same Jacksonians founded colleges with indefatigable zeal in the decades before the Civil War.

Dewey, too, saw himself as a Jeffersonian,[3] though he spent a good part of his life seeking to resolve certain dualisms that were at the very heart of the Jeffersonian view. Recall that Dewey came to American education as a critic, as a democrat deeply concerned over the failure of the schools to reach whole segments of the public and as a humanist deeply troubled by routinized procedures that seemed to stifle individuality and stultify growth. But instead of following Mann in stressing the equalitarian aspects of Jefferson's program as against the elitist, Dewey recast

[2] Horace Mann, *Lectures, and Annual Reports, on Education* (Cambridge, Mass.: Published for Mrs. Mary Mann, 1867), p. 315.

[3] See Dewey's introduction to *The Living Thoughts of Thomas Jefferson, Presented by John Dewey* (New York: Longmans, Green and Co., 1940).

the alternatives in a formulation so radical we have yet to apply it.

He sought first to dispel the idea that there is some sort of qualitative distinction between popular education on the one hand and leadership education on the other. "Democracy cannot flourish," he warned, "where the chief influences in selecting subject matter of instruction are utilitarian ends narrowly conceived for the masses, and, for the higher education of the few, the traditions of a specialized cultivated class." Where such influences are dominant, he went on to say, popular education becomes mechanical training in the three R's, while liberal education becomes "a somewhat parasitic cultivation bought at the expense of not having the enlightenment and discipline which come from concern with the deepest problems of common humanity." [4]

Dewey recognized that the creation of the common culture suggested here required the reconciliation of still another time-honored dualism, between culture on the one hand and everyday life on the other. Defining culture as "the capacity for constantly expanding the

[4] Dewey, *Democracy and Education*, p. 226.

range and accuracy of one's perception of meanings," Dewey saw the task of the educator as one of endowing ordinary human experience with intellectual, moral, and aesthetic significance.[5] In this view, the so-called cultural studies were cultural, not because of their remove from life, but because they represented the systematized and refined wisdom of the race.[6] No studies were inherently cultural; rather, a subject was cultural in the degree to which it was apprehended in its widest possible range of meanings. Hence, true culture could embrace a much larger group of subjects than had traditionally been the case, including even the trades and the practical arts if these were taught with the goal of growth in mind.[7]

Dewey's resolution is not without its problems, among them, the continuing difficulty of establishing curricular priorities and the crucial necessity of obtaining vast numbers of artist-teachers who are at the same time in-

[5] *Ibid.*, p. 145. There is an inescapable similarity to Whitehead's definition in *The Aims of Education* (New York: The Macmillan Co., 1929), p. 1: "Culture is activity of thought, and receptiveness to beauty and humane feeling."

[6] Dewey, *Democracy and Education*, pp. 212-16.

[7] *Ibid.*, Chap. 15.

formed scholars and imaginative pedagogues. Yet the resolution does lead to a concept of universal schooling that holds out to every human being the possibility of continuing his education throughout his lifetime and of systematically pursuing enhanced meaning in every realm of experience.

Be that as it may, the Deweyan view has been under sharp attack in recent years, from at least two quite different sources. First, there are those who believe that education for all is inescapably education for none and that the only realistic alternative is to concentrate on preparing the intellectually talented for positions of leadership.[8] Then, there are those who would divide humanity into two, three, or four strata of "giftedness" and design a fundamentally different curriculum for each group —different in substance as well as in approach, I might add.[9] Strange as it may seem, some of

[8] Douglas Bush, "Education for All Is Education for None," *New York Times Magazine,* January 9, 1955, pp. 13, 30-2.
[9] I refer, of course, to "life-adjustment education." See, for example, United States Office of Education, Division of Secondary Education and Division of Vocational Education, *Life Adjustment Education for Every Youth* (Washington, D.C.: Federal Security Agency, Office of Education, 1951) and Commission on Life Adjustment

these latter people actually think of themselves as intellectual heirs of Dewey, despite the fact that they too end up dividing the world into leaders and followers.

Quite apart from whether such approaches are Deweyan, they are certainly unwise. On the basis of prudence alone, no modern in-

Education for Youth, *Vitalizing Secondary Education* (Washington, D.C.: Federal Security Agency, Office of Education, 1951). In *The Revolution in Education* (Chicago: University of Chicago Press, 1958), Mortimer J. Adler and Milton Mayer classify most contemporary positions on the goals of American education into three "irreducible oppositions": *aristocratic* vs. *democratic, realist* vs. *idealist,* and *traditionalist* vs. *modernist.* The present-day *aristocrat,* unlike his ideological ancestors, holds that all men are equal as persons, but he firmly denies that more than a few are capable of education; his *democratic* opponent insists that all men are educable. *Democrats* themselves, however, divide into two camps: *democratic realists* urge that education must be differentiated, particularly at the high school level, to meet the needs of youngsters with varying abilities and vocational goals; *democratic idealists* flatly deny that any such differentiation is necessary. Finally, *democratic idealists* themselves split, the *traditionalists* among them insisting that the best education for all men still consists in the cultivation of intellect, the refinement of taste, and the development of character, the *modernists* arguing that vocational concerns can no longer be excluded from liberal education. One can criticize the classification (see my review in the *Progressive,* XXII [August, 1958], 28-9), but it is nonetheless useful. We might say, for example, that Dewey, as a *democratic idealist,* has been under attack from both *aristocrats* and *democratic realists.*

dustrial nation can fail to afford every one of
its citizens a maximum opportunity for intellectual and moral development. And beyond prudence, there is justice. No society
that calls itself democratic can settle for an
education that does not encourage universal
acquaintance with the best that has been
thought and said. This era, Arnold Toynbee
has remarked, is the first since the dawn of
civilization in which it is possible to provide
appreciable cultural benefits for the whole of
the human race. The possibility, Toynbee
continues, carries with it "a moral command
to execute the act of justice that is now at
last within our power." [10] Any lesser goal,
it seems to me, is narrow and unlovely, and
ultimately destructive of democracy.

2

"There is much of utter triviality of subject-
matter in elementary and secondary education," Dewey wrote in 1899. "When we in-

[10] Arnold J. Toynbee, "Conclusions," in Edward D.
Myers, *Education in the Perspective of History* (New
York: Harper & Brothers, 1960), p. 274.

vestigate it, we find that it is full of facts taught that are not facts, which have to be unlearned later on. Now, this happens because the 'lower' parts of our system are not in vital connection with the 'higher.' The university or college, in its idea, is a place of research, where investigation is going on, a place of libraries and museums, where the best resources of the past are gathered, maintained and organized. It is, however, as true in the school as in the university that the spirit of inquiry can be got only through and with the attitude of inquiry. The pupil must learn what has meaning, what enlarges his horizon, instead of mere trivialities. He must become acquainted with truths, instead of things that were regarded as such fifty years ago, or that are taken as interesting by the misunderstanding of a partially educated teacher. It is difficult to see how these ends can be reached except as the most advanced part of the educational system is in complete interaction with the most rudimentary." [11]

Dewey's comments suggest one of the chief problems in any viable theory of popular edu-

[11] John Dewey, *The School and Society* (Chicago: University of Chicago Press, 1899), pp. 92-3.

cation: the problem of popularizing culture, or, as James Harvey Robinson once phrased it, of humanizing knowledge so as to make it comprehensible to the average man.[12] The problem is inextricably tied to the so-called explosion of knowledge during the past half-century. Given the nature of scientific inquiry and its insistent pressure toward ever greater degrees of specialization, knowledge tends to become fragmented and dehumanized. Communities of scholars proliferate into subcommunities; fields of study are divided and subdivided; research problems are broken into subproblems, which then become the special concerns of subgroups within the several disciplines. The result is not two cultures, as C. P. Snow has suggested, but an infinite number of cultures, or, as I should prefer to phrase

[12] James Harvey Robinson, *The Humanizing of Knowledge* (New York: George H. Doran Co., 1923). Recall also Whitehead's incisive observation in *The Aims of Education* (p. 10): "There is only one subject-matter for education, and that is Life in all its manifestations. Instead of this single unity, we offer children—Algebra, from which nothing follows; Geometry, from which nothing follows; Science, from which nothing follows; History, from which nothing follows; a Couple of Languages, never mastered; and lastly, most dreary of all, Literature, represented by plays of Shakespeare, with philological notes and short analyses of plot and character to be in substance committed to memory."

49

it, an infinite number of subdivisions within one culture. The task of the educator is to rehumanize knowledge, to resynthesize and reorder it in some way that will render it teachable.

I think it fair to say that this task of rehumanizing, resynthesizing, and reordering knowledge was the central problem facing the early progressives in building a new curriculum for the nation's schools and colleges. It gave rise to the celebrated general education courses developed at Chicago and Columbia during the 1920's, and it stimulated the new elementary and secondary school programs in the social studies, the language arts, and the natural sciences that we have come to associate with the progressive education movement. Yet something happened during the 1920's that doomed the effort to failure. The story is long and involved, and I have dealt with it in other writings. Suffice it here to say that the problems were partly ideological (the view that to lay out a curriculum in advance is somehow undemocratic, or the assumption that a youngster who has trouble with history can just as well spend his time in shop) and partly political (the decision of the newly self-conscious teaching profession to separate itself from the academic scholars in the colleges and universities). In any case, as early as 1928, Dewey used his presidential address to the Progressive Education Association to chastise his fellow educators for destroying better than they built, for throwing out traditional curricula without substituting new curricula that structured and ordered knowledge more effectively.[13] It was a charge that would be widely reiterated in the years following World War II.

[13] "Progressive Education and the Science of Education," *Progressive Education*, V (1928), 197-204. That growth, as Dewey conceived it, requires systematic study of the disciplines is patent from his discussions in *How We Think* (Boston: D. C. Heath & Co., 1910), pp. 56-67, 135-44, 157-87; *Interest and Effort in Education* (Boston: Houghton Mifflin Co., 1913), pp. 81-4; and *Experience and Education* (New York: The Macmillan Co., 1938). It should be noted, however, that Dewey conceived of the disciplines, not as static or complete, but as constantly subject to revision, expansion, and reorganization on the basis of new discoveries and empirical testing. The Deweyan program, as Dr. and Mrs. Dewey institutionalized it in the Laboratory School at the University of Chicago between 1896 and 1903, is also revealing. See Katherine Camp Mayhew and Anna Camp Edwards, *The Dewey School* (New York: D. Appleton-Century Co., 1936). The unwillingness of the Deweys to merge the school with the Francis W. Parker school after 1900 stemmed in part from their insistence upon continuing their experiments with revised curricula.

We are all familiar with the more recent curriculum reform movement that has generated such excitement among educators and the lay public.[14] Beginning with mathematics and the natural sciences, groups of teachers and scholars have gotten together to update and reconstitute syllabi and teaching materials in virtually every field of study. And they have made imaginative use of a vast variety of instructional devices, from simple film strips to computer-regulated teletype machines. The movement has provided a vital new thrust in education, and to the extent that it has been tied to teacher-training institutes, it has evolved a mechanism not only for updating what now goes on in the schools but for continually updating what will go on in the future. I have no doubt that in years to come teachers in our popular school system —and I would include most college professors in that category—will be returning regularly to university centers to extend their own knowledge at the same time as they consider new ways of organizing and synthesizing the materials in their fields.

[14] See Robert W. Heath, ed., *The New Curricula* (New York: Harper & Row, 1964).

My point, of course, is that the current curriculum reform movement must be seen as essentially continuous with the efforts of the early progressives. This is not to say that the pedagogical assumptions of the two movements are identical: while there are patent continuities between Dewey's *How We Think* (1910) and Bruner's *The Process of Education* (1960), there are differences too, and these must be reckoned with if one is to comprehend what is new about the new curricula.[15] But the ultimate aim of both reform efforts is the same: to humanize knowledge so that it can be popularized.

For this very reason, however, I think a number of considerations must be faced if the contemporary movement is to achieve maximum effect. First, the new reformers have

[15] One of the most intriguing features of Bruner's work —and I think one explanation for its profound influence —is that it draws not only from Dewey but from Whitehead as well. Thus, for example, Bruner's ideas of "structure" and the "discovery method" stem directly from Whitehead, while his idea of "spiraling" is closely related to Whitehead's idea of "periodicity," the "conveyance of difference within a framework of repetition." Charles Silberman has indicated in a number of unpublished manuscripts the extent to which present-day curriculum innovators seem to be "going back to Whitehead."

taken as their motto Bruner's oft-quoted assertion "that any subject can be taught effectively
in some intellectually honest form to any child
at any stage of development." [16] The principle
has been a useful one in clearing the air of a
lot of nonsense about "readiness"; for as Bruner and others have pointed out, the idea of
readiness is itself a "mischievous half-truth,"
since one teaches readiness at least as much as
one waits for it.[17] Yet however liberating Bruner's principle has been, it has merely liberated
us to begin the determination of what ought
to be taught to children at any given stage.
There is no avoiding the question of purpose;
and given the limited time children spend in
school and the growing influence of other educational agencies, we have to ask Spencerian
questions more insistently than ever: What
knowledge is of most worth? What priorities
in education?

Second, whereas Dewey's generation of reformers assumed that knowledge would have
to be "psychologized" to be made teachable,
the present generation of reformers has in-

[16] Jerome S. Bruner, *The Process of Education* (Cambridge, Mass.: Harvard University Press, 1960), p. 33.
[17] Jerome S. Bruner, "Education as Social Invention,"
Journal of Social Issues, XX (1964), 27.

sisted that intellectual activity is everywhere the same, whether at the frontier of research or in a third-grade classroom. "The schoolboy learning physics *is* a physicist," Bruner tells us, "and it is easier for him to learn physics behaving like a physicist than doing something else." Both views reflect a concern with conveying meaning; both recognize that there is too much to be learned to permit preoccupation with isolated bits of information. But Bruner's dictum, if misunderstood, could easily lead educators to the unfortunate conclusion that knowledge does not have to be recast at all for purposes of teaching. What is needed more than ever, it seems to me, is systematic testing of all new curricular programs and continuing experiment with a variety of approaches to each field of study. Only by insisting on such experiment and testing shall we avoid a new academic formalism that could easily become as Procrustean as the formalism against which the progressives themselves first revolted.[18]

[18] The quotation is from Bruner, *The Process of Education*, p. 14. Note the pertinent analysis of "the mission-discipline duality" in Alvin M. Weinberg, "But Is the Teacher Also a Citizen?" *Science*, CXLIX (August 6, 1965), 601-6.

Third, and closely related here, the new reformers have been consistently ambivalent on the question of pedagogy. They have rightly attacked a good deal of contemporary teaching as dull, uninformed, and unimaginative; and they have properly emphasized teacher training as a crucial component of their programs. But too often, their teacher training has been just that: training in the mechanical use of a particular set of materials rather than education in the intelligent use of all available materials. Indeed, some of the reformers have actually advanced the heady idea of eventually producing "teacher-proof" materials, so tightly and artistically constructed as to be impervious to misuse by ill-trained instructors. I think I know what motivates them: progressive education, after all, demanded infinitely skilled teachers, and it failed because such teachers could not be recruited in sufficient numbers. Some of the contemporary reformers are determined not to go wrong on the same score. Now, there is no denying that teachers must be technically competent, and the reformers have not only the right but the obligation to produce careful and detailed strategies for the use of their materials. (N. L. Gage has even put forth the intriguing suggestion that we develop a standard "choreography" for noting pedagogical prescriptions.) But education is too significant and dynamic an enterprise to be left to mere technicians; and we might as well begin now the prodigious task of preparing men and women who understand not only the substance of what they are teaching but also the theories behind the particular strategies they employ to convey that substance. A society committed to the continuing intellectual, aesthetic, and moral growth of all its members can ill afford less on the part of those who undertake to teach.

Fourth, there is no avoiding the fact that the new reformers have approached their task piecemeal and with little concern for the curriculum as a whole. This derives partly from the organization of the academic disciplines within the university, from which, after all, the principal thrust of the new reform has come, and partly from the pattern of support from the chief funding agencies, notably the National Science Foundation. The assumption, it seems to me, is that the curriculum is essentially the sum of its parts, and that once all the individual academic subjects are under review, the task of curriculum development is well launched. In some respects, of course, this is entirely valid; no generalist can be expert in every field, and I suspect that a good deal of the intellectual flabbiness of school curricula in the 1940's and 1950's derived from an overdose of generalism. Even so, someone must look at the curriculum whole and raise insistent questions of priority and relationship. Education is more than a succession of units, courses, and programs, however excellent; and to refuse to look at curricula in their entirety is to relegate to intraschool politics a series of decisions that ought to call into play the most fundamental philosophical principles. Incidentally, having made this point, I should add that no one individual can or should be solely responsible for this concern, but it must certainly be the leading business of anyone who fancies himself a principal, a president, or a dean.

Finally, there is the thorny question of class bias. The new reformers have frequently been labeled elitists, whose principal concern is the gifted child on his way to college. Now, it is quite true that a number of the more successful reform programs were begun in an effort to develop more stimulating intellectual fare for bright youngsters; but I think the charge of elitism is generally unfounded. The ultimate commitment of the new reformers is to producing a common culture of high quality for all American youngsters. They simply refuse to honor the view that only twenty percent of our children can profit from academic courses and that the remaining eighty percent need either trade training or something called "life adjustment education." Indeed, their real contention is that all children need the "new math" and the "new English" if they are to make any intelligent adjustment whatsoever to modern life. This is not to say that they are foolish enough to argue that every child can master the sciences and the humanities in exactly the same way; it is rather to say that they are radical enough to argue that every child can master the sciences and the humanities in some intellectually honest way. Once again, the new reformers are far closer to the original spirit of Dewey in this respect than many of his self-styled disciples, though it must be added that their sharpest challenge still lies ahead of them, namely, to design up-to-date curricula that make no compromise with truth or significance and yet prove attractive and comprehensible to dull or poorly motivated children.

H. G. Wells was fond of asserting that modern man is engaged in a race between education and catastrophe. I think that race has become more difficult and more significant than Wells ever knew. The demands on today's American who would be Jefferson's responsible citizen are virtually overwhelming. Some years ago, when President Kennedy was debating whether to call a halt to atomic testing, James Reston devoted a column to the problem posed for citizens.[19] Some scientists were contending that atomic fallout would do untold harm to unborn generations of children; others, equally well reputed, were arguing that such claims were gross exaggerations. Kennedy was faced with the lonely task of reaching some sort of decision, and Reston was not unappreciative of his burden. But sooner or later, Reston pointed out, the average American would have to judge the wisdom of Kennedy's decision. Jefferson's faith—and the faith on which any democracy must rest— was that the average man, properly educated,

[19] *New York Times,* March 7, 1962, p. 34.

could indeed render such a judgment. There are those of good will who long ago abandoned that faith. I happen to affirm it, though the tasks it sets for education are nothing short of herculean.

3

The case for a common culture at the heart of Dewey's theory of education is inextricably tied to his theory of democracy. Like Mann before him, Dewey clearly recognized that education is a matter of individual growth and development; but like Mann, too, he was deeply sensitive to the need for social integration, and he pressed insistently for the sort of common schooling that would bring the children of all classes, creeds, and ethnic backgrounds into little "embryonic communities." This should hardly be surprising, given his definition of democracy as "primarily a mode of associated living."

Actually, by the time Dewey came upon the educational scene, the common school had achieved something of a triumph in the United

States, and was widely perceived, both at home and abroad, as providing the cement that held the American body politic together. Indeed, a steady stream of foreign observers felt moved to remark upon the phenomenon. Francis Adams, for example, secretary of the English National Education League, noted in 1875: "One of the most remarkable features of the American free school is its almost infinite power of assimilation, and this is one of the greatest works which the school does. It draws children from all nations together, and marks them with the impress of nationality." [20] And twenty-eight years later, the Reverend T. L. Papillon, a member of the celebrated Mosely Educational Commission, observed: "The 'common' schools are, as anyone who sees them at work can tell, a great unifying force in the life of the nation, always engaged in stamping a mass of heterogeneous elements with the hall-mark of American citizenship. Whatever else they teach, they teach patriotism and some knowledge of civic duty. . . ." [21]

[20] Francis Adams, *The Free School System of the United States* (London: Chapman and Hall, 1875), p. 94.
[21] *Reports of the Mosely Educational Commission to the United States of America* (London: Co-operative Printing Society, 1904), p. 250.

Now, as a historian I am not quite sure how one would go about estimating the precise integrative power of the common schools. What should not be discounted, however, is the prodigious influence of the *belief* that common schooling unifies. For one thing, it generated the kind of political support for public education that could and did easily cross class lines. And for another, it led educators to attempt to make the schools ever more attractive to widely disparate social groups. Yet granted this, I think we need to look much more closely than we have in the past at the variant forms in which the common school appeared and at those situations in which it failed to appear at all.

My own studies have led me to the hypothesis that the common school in its classic form was essentially a Northern and Western phenomenon and that it reached its apotheosis in rural and small-town America west of the Alleghenies. It thrived best where there was already a reasonable homogeneity of race, class, and religion, and where communities were not so large as to permit the development of substantially dissimilar ghettos. Wherever social or physical distances did become great, as in the South or in the larger cities, the public school tended to be less "common." [22] Thus, at the very time Dewey

[22] Bishop James Fraser of Manchester, England, actually noted this in his 1866 report to the Schools Inquiry Commissions: "By the theory of a common school system scholars of every rank are supposed to come within the sphere of its operation. But actual—I don't know whether they can be called natural—distinctions cannot be disposed of by a theory, and, as a matter of fact, social distinctions do tell with a very marked effect upon American schools. Speaking generally, they are in possession of the great middle class, the artizans, store-keepers, farmers. The system works with a much nearer approach to its *idea* or theoretic perfection in the country, where ranks are more equalized, and there is no one rich and no one poor, than it does in the cities and towns. Yet even in country districts 'aristocratic feelings' and prejudices, very foolishly and unhappily, it must be admitted, are beginning to prevail. And in all the cities, New York, Newhaven [sic], Hartford, Providence, and even in Boston, the wealthier class, indeed all who can afford to do so, almost without exception, send their children to private schools. Of the persons whose acquaintance I made in the country, most of whom I should rate at about the same level of social rank and social feeling as myself, I do not remember one who used either for sons or daughters the common schools. In all these cities there are finishing schools for young ladies just as there would be in cities of the same character among ourselves; and there are private day or boarding schools for boys, at which they remain till they are fit for college" (*Report to the Commissioners Appointed by Her Majesty to Inquire into the Education Given in Schools in England Not Comprised within Her Majesty's Two Recent Commissions, and to the Commissioners Appointed by Her Majesty to Inquire into the Schools in Scotland, on the Common School System of the United States and of the Provinces of*

was developing his idea of the school as an inclusive "embryonic community," the newly enfranchised Negroes of the South were being systematically barred from access to common schools (often, incidentally, with Progressive support);[23] Roman Catholics were responding to the hierarchy's decision to create a place for every Catholic child in a Catholic school;[24] and the upper classes in the larger cities of the East were either sending their children to private schools or, through residential segregation, creating public schools that were not common schools.[25] This last ac-

Upper and Lower Canada [London: Her Majesty's Stationery Office, 1866], pp. 97-100).

[23] See John Hope Franklin, "Jim Crow Goes to School: The Genesis of Legal Segregation in Southern Schools," *South Atlantic Quarterly*, LVIII (1959), 225-35; Louis R. Harlan, *Separate and Unequal* (Chapel Hill, N.C.: University of North Carolina Press, 1958); and C. Vann Woodward, *The Strange Career of Jim Crow* (New York: Oxford University Press, 1955).

[24] Neil G. McCluskey, ed., *Catholic Education in America: A Documentary History* (New York: Bureau of Publications, Teachers College, Columbia University, 1964) and Daniel F. Reilly, *The School Controversy (1891-1893)* (Washington, D.C.: Catholic University of America Press, 1943).

[25] The evidence here is at present fragmentary and frequently contradictory. See, for example, Fraser, *Report on the Common School System*, pp. 97-100, and Adams, *The Free School System of the United States*, pp. 86-95. What is interesting is the tendency of Fraser and Adams to "discover" American evidence to support

tion, interestingly enough, did give rise to one celebrated version of the common school— the single-class slum school that brought together immigrant children of different ethnic and religious backgrounds. The so-called flight from the cities of today's middle class in search of better public education is no new phenomenon; fifty years ago, the middle class simply moved "uptown" for the same reason. The principal difference is that "uptown" was still within the city limits, or was quickly made a part of the city through annexation.

We also need to bear in mind that although the dominant ideological commitment was to common schooling, there was never an absence of vigorous dissent. As early as 1830, the editor of the *National Gazette and Literary Register* reminded Pennsylvania school reformers that there would "ever be distinctions of condition,—of capacity,—of knowledge and ignorance,—in spite of all the fond conceits which may be indulged, or the wild projects which may be tried, to the contrary." [26] Opposition to common schooling on

the positions they were taking with respect to the future of English education.

[26] *National Gazette and Literary Register* [Philadelphia], July 10, 1830, p. [2].

religious grounds was widespread, coming not only from Roman Catholics but from certain Protestant groups as well, the argument being that the doctrinal compromise necessitated by a heterogeneous clientele undermined the very foundation of true education. And a number of ethnic groups—the Germans in Pennsylvania are an excellent example—resisted common schooling on the grounds that it precluded proper appreciation of Old World language and custom.

Opposition to racial mixing in the common schools was widely voiced in both the North and the South. "Let the children of the richest and poorest parents in the State, meet in the schoolroom on the terms of perfect equality of right," declared Governor Joseph E. Brown of Georgia in 1858. "Let there be no aristocracy there but an aristocracy of color and conduct." [27] And finally, there were the various arguments embodying social or intellectual considerations. Some people simply wanted no part of "class mixing" for their

[27] Clement Eaton, *Freedom of Thought in the Old South* (Durham, N.C.: Duke University Press, 1940), p. 74. See also Rush Welter, *Popular Education and Democratic Thought in America* (New York: Columbia University Press, 1962), Chap. 8.

youngsters; others, genuinely concerned over the poor quality of the public schools, placed their children in private schools rather than seeking to upgrade the educational programs that dissatisfied them.

All these arguments are very much with us today; indeed, they have engendered some of the most intractable political problems of our time. Thus, the civil rights struggle as it bears on education may be viewed as mainly a conflict over whether the ideal of common schooling shall extend to the nation's Negro children. The leading battles over Federal aid to education have long centered on the question of public funds for denominational schools, or, as a writer in the *Harvard Law Review* once put it, on whether parochial schools shall be encouraged.[28] And the bitter controversies over the reapportionment of our state legislatures stem at least in part from the gross disparities that have arisen between urban schools for the poor and suburban schools for the well-to-do.[29]

[28] *Harvard Law Review*, LX (1947), 800.
[29] See James B. Conant, *Slums and Suburbs* (New York: McGraw-Hill Book Co., 1961).

We have tended to argue these issues legal-istically in recent years, returning again and again to the constitutionality of this or that proposal. But at bottom, these are issues of pub-lic policy, and they should be considered and debated as such. What is ultimately at stake, it seems to me, is the social orientation of American popular schooling; and we cannot talk about that orientation without having some sense of the kind of America the schools will help bring into being.

In this respect, it is interesting to contem-plate two quite different views and the bear-ing they have on educational policy. First, there is the picture of America given in Will Herberg's celebrated *Protestant-Catholic-Jew* (1955). Those who accept Herberg's position that the religious revival of the past twenty years represents a healthy flight from con-formity, and who would welcome the three Americanisms he sees as inevitable outcomes of this revival, are raising some searching ques-tions about the whole commitment to the common school. Actually, they propose the establishment of several "public school" sys-tems, each under the auspices of a different denomination, the goal being a more diverse and pluralistic American life.[30] Whatever the validity of the unspoken assumptions concerning the power of schooling to generate social homogeneity or heterogeneity, the arguments themselves doubtless have their influence on public policy.

Have we, in fact, become so much alike that we need to create new patterns of public schooling to promote diversity? The evidence is contradictory. Thus, in opposition to Herberg's view, we have the one presented by Nathan Glazer and Daniel Moynihan in *Beyond the Melting Pot* (1963), a study of eth-

[30] Herberg actually advanced such a view in *America*, XCVIII (November 16, 1957), 190-93, and in John Cogley, ed., *Religion in America* (New York: Meridian Books, 1958), pp. 118-47. Herberg's assumptions about the diversifying effects of denominational education are sharply challenged by the criticism Roman Catholics themselves are leveling at the parochial schools. See the reports of addresses at the April 1965 convention of the National Catholic Educational Association in the *New York Times*, April 21, 1965, p. 35, April 23, 1965, p. 31, and April 24, 1965, pp. 1, 32; and Emmet John Hughes's incisive commentary in *Newsweek*, LXV (May 3, 1965), 21. See also the preliminary reports of the National Opinion Research Center study of the effects of Catholic education in *The Critic* for December, 1963-January, 1964, for October-November, 1964, and for February-March, 1965.

nic and religious politics in New York City. The Glazer-Moynihan picture, recognizable to anyone who has taken part in the political life of a large city, is one of continuing inter-group hostility and suspicion, requiring the constant renewal of whatever slender basis there is for the resolution of tension and conflict. To accept this view is to acknowledge with greater conviction than ever the need for certain common educational experiences of the sort Mann and Dewey were so eager to provide. (Incidentally, I would interject that one can accept the implications of the Glazer-Moynihan view without in any way minimizing the dangers of conformity. The commitment to common schooling need not preclude the devotion to uncommon men; it merely recognizes that uncommon men also live in communities.)

I myself am led to the conclusion that the nurture of a common culture remains a central task of American popular education, and that the common school continues to stand as a prime agency for undertaking this task. But I am led also to observe that there are other agencies that can—and do—contribute signif-

icantly to the common education of the public, and that it is a serious error to discuss the
problem without paying heed to the new opportunities they afford. The importance of
radio and television, and the common experiences they provide, cannot be overestimated.
And certainly the provisions in the Elementary and Secondary Education Act of 1965
for supplementary education centers, common
textbooks, and shared-time programs offer ex-
citing new possibilities for developing common educational enterprises under public
sponsorship. Again, the point is to bear in
mind the totality of popular education.

One final matter requires comment here;
Dewey dealt with it in *Democracy and Education*. "Is it possible," he asked, "for an educational system to be conducted by a national
state and yet the full social ends of the educative process not be restricted, constrained,
and corrupted?" He was raising, of course, the
question of how to reconcile national loyalty
with "superior devotion to the things which
unite men in common ends, irrespective of national political boundaries." [31] The problem is

[31] Dewey, *Democracy and Education,* pp. 113-14.

a very old one, but it has taken on new significance with the development of modern forms of communication and warfare. The fact is that the same disparities in educational aspiration and attainment that corrode democracy within nations also corrode democracy among nations, and certainly no common culture that stops at national borders can be adequate in the contemporary world. How we set in motion the dialogue essential to the development of an international culture remains to be seen. The experience of UNESCO is at best mixed, though UNESCO has managed to go significantly beyond its predecessor, the League of Nations' Intellectual Cooperation Organization.[32] Suffice it to say that no world political system or world legal system can long endure apart from the development

---

[32] Compare I. L. Kandel, *Intellectual Cooperation: National and International* (New York: Bureau of Publications, Teachers College, Columbia University, 1944) with Walter H. C. Laves and Charles A. Thomson, *UNESCO: Purpose, Progress, Prospects* (Bloomington, Ind.: Indiana University Press, 1957). See also David G. Scanlon, ed., *International Education: A Documentary History* (New York: Bureau of Publications, Teachers College, Columbia University, 1962); *Humanism and Education in East and West* (Paris: United Nations Educational, Scientific and Cultural Organization, 1953); and Robert Ulich, ed., *Education and the Idea of Mankind* (New York: Harcourt, Brace & World, 1964).

of a viable international culture. Whether or not wars begin in the minds of men, that is where they must end, as men deliberately opt for other methods of resolving their differences.

4

Ultimately, the case for popular education rests on the proposition that culture can be democratized without being vulgarized. It is a radical proposition that flies in the face of two thousand years of Western wisdom to the effect that true culture demands an elite. And it is a proposition that must really be accepted on faith, since the whole idea of a democratic culture is too new to have stood the test of time.

Actually, those who launched our experiment in popular schooling were little troubled by the problem. If anything, there is a wonderfully childlike optimism about their programs. "The State which teaches one new truth to one of its citizens does something," Horace Mann observed in 1842; "but how much more, when, by teaching that truth to all, it multiplies its utilities and its pleasures by the number of all its citizens." [33] The world's wisdom, formerly reserved for kings, priests, and nobles, would at last be made available to the people at large; and the result could only be a golden age of progress, unparalleled in history.

There have always been skeptics, of course; but it is my impression that the optimism generated by Mann and his contemporaries lasted well into the twentieth century, certainly through the initial phase of the progressive education movement. Then, something of a shift occurred that has been fashionably referred to as the passing of modernism. It is not easy to date, but it appears to have taken place during the 1930's, in close connection with a number of profound historical changes. First, an economic depression of unprecedented severity held the entire Western world in its grip. Second, the so-called popular dictatorships were moving rapidly into their totalitarian stages, and thought control and concentration camps were emerging in the most

[33] Mann, *Lectures, and Annual Reports, on Education*, p. 312.

literate and "cultured" nations of the world. Third, the products of mass journalism, radio, and cinema were becoming increasingly visible to intellectuals, and increasingly distressing. Fourth, pessimistic but persuasive explanations of what was happening began to appear in a number of works, chief among them, José Ortega y Gasset's *The Revolt of the Masses* (1932). And finally, the gulf between the leaders of the popular school system and those of the intellectual community at large continued to widen. I have always thought it indicative of the shift that the same Walter Lippmann who in 1916 acclaimed *Democracy and Education* as "the mature wisdom of the finest and most powerful intellect devoted to the future of American civilization" felt impelled a quarter of a century later to lash out scathingly against what he deemed the shoddiness and superficiality of the modern school.[34]

Now, as Leo Lowenthal, Raymond Williams, and others have pointed out, pessimism and optimism with regard to popular culture

[34] Walter Lippmann, "The Hope of Democracy," *New Republic*, VII (1916), 231, and "Education without Culture," *Commonweal*, XXXIII (1940-41), 323.

have long and parallel histories, dating from the emergence of printed popular literature in the sixteenth and seventeenth centuries.[35] We are all familiar with the issue as it is joined today. Consider the argument of Dwight Macdonald, probably the leading contemporary exponent of the pessimist view. "The historical reasons for the growth of Mass Culture since the early 1800's are well known," Macdonald tells us. "Political democracy and popular education broke down the old upper-class monopoly of culture. Business enterprise found a profitable market in the cultural demands of the newly awakened masses, and the advance of technology made possible the cheap production of books, periodicals, pictures, music, and furniture, in sufficient quantities to satisfy this market. Modern technology also created new media such as the movies and television which are especially well

[35] Leo Lowenthal, "Historical Perspectives of Popular Culture," *American Journal of Sociology*, LV (1950), 323-32; Leo Lowenthal and Marjorie Fiske, "The Debate over Art and Popular Culture in Eighteenth Century England," in Mirra Komarovsky, ed., *Common Frontiers of the Social Sciences* (Glencoe, Ill.: The Free Press, 1957), pp. 33-112; and Raymond Williams, *Culture and Society* (London: Chatto & Windus, 1958) and *The Long Revolution* (London: Chatto & Windus, 1961).

adapted to mass manufacture and distribution." As a result, Macdonald continues, certain elements of high culture and mass culture merged, yielding a tepid, flaccid "midcult," stylized, mass-produced for profit, and ultimately corruptive of the talents of its creators. Since "midcult" is essentially a manufactured commodity rather than an art form, it tends always downward, toward cheapness and standardization.[36]

Those who hold a more optimistic view are no less critical of much that passes for popular culture. If we take Gilbert Seldes as an example, the argument is certainly not that popular culture has been an unqualified success; on the contrary, Seldes has been as sharply critical as anyone of the cheap sensationalism and slick uniformity of much that is proffered by the media.[37] But Seldes does go

[36] Dwight Macdonald, "A Theory of Mass Culture," *Diogenes*, No. 3 (Summer, 1953), pp. 1-17, and also *Against the American Grain* (New York: Random House, 1962), pp. 3-75.

[37] Gilbert Seldes, *The Great Audience* (New York: The Viking Press, 1950) and *The Public Arts* (New York: Simon and Schuster, 1956). Seldes indicates his differences with Macdonald in *The Great Audience*, pp. 250-64. For a more recent critique of Macdonald, see Alvin Toffler, *The Culture Consumers* (New York: St. Martin's Press, 1964). A fundamental optimism also

on to make two fundamental points. First, he justifiably indicates that the record of the media is mixed, that the same television networks that narcotize with soap opera also elevate with Shakespeare. Thus, it is significant to recall that more people saw *Hamlet* on a single night over television than have seen it in live performances since it was written.[38] True, not everyone appreciated *Hamlet* at the same level; but to have brought Shakespeare to that number of people in no way cheapened Shakespeare. Second, Seldes argues that it is certainly not foreordained that popular culture must be sensational and sordid. If some artists have made their peace with "the system," not all have done so; indeed, some have produced significant new work as a result of the opportunities afforded by the media.[39]

suffuses the Rockefeller Panel Report published under the title *The Performing Arts: Problems and Prospects* (New York: McGraw-Hill Book Co., 1965).

[38] Frank Stanton, *Mass Media and Mass Culture* (New York: Columbia Broadcasting System, 1962), p. 35.

[39] Seldes, *The Great Audience*, pp. 263-64. In this argument, Seldes comes close to Marshall McLuhan's position that a change in the nature of the medium works a transforming influence on the substance of the message. See McLuhan, *The Gutenberg Galaxy* (Toronto: University of Toronto Press, 1962) and *Understanding Media* (New York: McGraw-Hill Book Co., 1964).

In the end, I think the argument between the pessimists and the optimists is essentially a historical one: it concerns the idea of "the masses" and the character of their traditional culture. Some years ago, in a perceptive review of *Mass Culture* (1957) by Bernard Rosenberg and David Manning White, Edward Shils pointed out that pessimists who contend that modern popular culture has debased the masses have a roseate view of what the culture of the masses was before the media came into existence.[40] The often unstated assumption is that an inherently cheap mass culture gradually replaced an inherently fine folk culture. But if one examines the life of farming and working people before the advent of popular culture, one finds less of a rich folk culture than of a dull, humdrum existence interspersed with moments of gross and tawdry entertainment. Modern soap opera, Shils concluded, is the successor, not of folk ballads or Shakespeare, but of bearbaiting and public executions.

And beyond this, there is a point to be

[40] Edward Shils, "Daydreams and Nightmares: Reflections on the Criticism of Mass Culture," *Sewanee Review*, LXV (1957), 587-608.

made concerning the very concept of "the masses." When one speaks of "masses," as opposed to "people" or "publics," the term itself becomes a device for justifying cheap sensationalism and crass commercialism.[41] The artist—or the educator—who offers the public pap, insisting that pap is what the public wants, is telling us less about the public than about his own conception of his work. And here we return to the relationship between popular education and popular culture. If culture is, as Dewey suggested, "the capacity for constantly expanding the range and accuracy of one's perception of meanings," then the popular media must be judged by the extent to which their fare enhances this capacity in individual men and women, or, stated another way, by the extent to which they further participation in a genuine popular culture.

We come back, obviously, not merely to the sense of educational purpose in the society at large but also to the commitment of the professionals entrusted with operating the

[41] The term also becomes one of social and political denigration. See David Spitz, *Patterns of Anti-Democratic Thought* (New York: The Macmillan Co., 1949), Chap. 4.

media and the political and economic con-
trols under which they work. If the public is
willing to grant that the ultimate purpose of
television is to sell soap, cigarettes, and cereal,
and if the professional sees his task as one of
lulling audiences into insensibility so that they
will buy soap, cigarettes, and cereal, then the
society will get the kind of culture it deserves.
But if the public were to insist that the broadcaster's ultimate responsibility is to educate,
then a far different popular culture would
result.

It would be easy here to fall into the Pla-
tonic fallacy that the only solution is public
control of all the agencies that educate; this,
after all, is precisely how totalitarian societies
solve the problem. What the public *can* do, it
seems to me, both within the schools and
without, is sponsor intellectual and aesthetic
alternatives that are excellent. I have no illu-
sion that such alternatives will immediately
wean vast audiences from the sort of entertainment that appears to enchant them today.
But the evidence indicates that they will at-
tract large numbers of people. And in a free
society, that attraction is all that can be
counted on. To Macdonald's contention that

the cheap will inevitably drive out the good, I would counterpose the classical dictum that the way to nurture taste is to make the good so widely available that the cheap ceases to satisfy.[42] In the last analysis, the function of the popular educator is to make certain that the good is there to contemplate.

[42] Sir Richard Livingstone advanced this view in *The Rainbow Bridge* (London: Pall Mall Press, 1959), Chap. 1, as did Walter Kerr in *The Decline of Pleasure* (New York: Simon and Schuster, 1962), Chap. 7.

III

The Politics of

Popular Education

THE POLITICAL PHILOSOPHY OF Thomas Jefferson rests on two fundamental assumptions: that the end of life is individual happiness and that the purpose of government is to secure and advance that happiness. Since education in Jefferson's view is the firmest foundation of happiness, it clearly becomes the foremost function of government. Hence, the state must sponsor education for all to the extent that each is capable of profiting from it; and the state must control that education as "the most certain, and the most legitimate engine of government." [1] This last principle is patently reflected in the bills of 1779 by the provision that the primary schools be locally managed by representatives of the public and that the College of William and Mary be run by a board ultimately responsible to the legislature.

As is well known, Jefferson's own triumph was the founding of the University of Virginia. But it was rather in the commercial North than the agrarian South that his principles regarding universal education were best realized.[2] And it was not until the Southern state university was later joined to the Northern common school in the newer states of the Midwest that the whole of his plan was finally

[1] Enclosure with Thomas Jefferson to Uriah Forrest, December 31, 1787, in Julian P. Boyd, ed., *The Papers of Thomas Jefferson* (Princeton, N.J.: Princeton University Press, 1950-), XII, 478. See also Charles Maurice Wiltse, *The Jeffersonian Tradition in American Democracy* (Chapel Hill, N.C.: University of North Carolina Press, 1935), pp. 139-44.

[2] The common assumption, however, that the pre-Civil War South made little or no progress toward universal education is simply not valid. See Forrest David Mathews, "The Politics of Education in the Deep South: Georgia and Alabama, 1830-1860" (Unpublished doctoral thesis, Teachers College, Columbia University, 1965).

adopted. The foremost example, of course, was Michigan, where the fathers of the state simply wedded the Jeffersonian "Catholepistemiad" and the New England common school to form the so-called ladder system that has since characterized American public education.

Horace Mann's generation not only built firmly on Jeffersonian principles, it also went beyond them. Mann himself never tired of reminding the people of Massachusetts that support for education would have to begin at the local level. Without local support, no amount of imploring from Boston would make a difference. But having repeated this Jeffersonian dictum, Mann urged two innovations: the location of partial control in state agencies and the professionalization of teaching.

The first, of course, was less an innovation than the reassertion of a prerogative that had earlier slipped away. For all of Jefferson's emphasis on local control, it was, after all, the Virginia legislature to which he had turned in his effort to effect educational improvement. All the colonial legislatures had pronounced on aspects of education in the seventeenth and eighteenth centuries, and the idea of legislative control was hardly new. Indeed, my colleague R. Freeman Butts has argued—and I think persuasively—that "education was one of the powers and rights of political sovereignty transferred to American shores by the charters, patents, and governmental regulations of the sovereigns of the mother countries." [3] Yet power over education had tended to slip into the hands of localities as settlers dispersed and new communities took form. In Massachusetts, as in other states, tremendous differences had developed in the ability and willingness of various communities to support schooling; and Mann saw in the reassertion of state prerogative the key to statewide educational improvement.

Mann's second innovation was the professionalization of teaching. This never became a problem for Jefferson, primarily, I think, because his bills of 1779 were never passed; and one searches his works in vain for any major pronouncements on the selection and training of teachers for the popular schools. Mann, on the other hand, shared Victor Cousin's con-

[3] R. Freeman Butts, "Our Tradition of States' Rights and Education," *History of Education Journal,* VI (1954-55), 213.

viction that as the teacher goes so goes the school; and he was firmly convinced that with all the popular interest in the world, Massachusetts would never have a first-rate education system without a first-rate corps of teachers. He therefore campaigned insistently for those conditions that would facilitate the creation of a teaching profession: careful selection of personnel, well-designed advanced training, and increased status and authority. He did not achieve his goal; and as late as 1898, only a third of the teachers of Massachusetts had graduated from even a normal school. But it is to Mann that we must look for some of the earliest and most persuasive arguments for the professionalization of American teaching.

The progressives pushed forward on both fronts, demanding more effective popular control on the one hand and more effective classroom teaching on the other. With regard to popular control, there was a characteristic shift in their position—from an earlier view in which education was to be rescued from "the interests" and restored to "the people," to a later (and I think more sophisticated) view in which "the interests" were recognized as articulate publics and the problem was seen as

one of getting all significant publics represented in policy-making. Thus, in 1928, George
S. Counts concluded a pioneering study of
School and Society in Chicago with the recommendation that "rather than seek refuge in
the cautious counsel of removing the school
from politics, we should move forward under
the assumption that the real business of politics
is to provide the channels through which the
living energies of society may flow into new
forms and patterns. The great desideratum
. . . is to devise some means of making the
school responsive to the more fundamental
social realities and of enabling it at the same
time to maintain an even keel amid the clash
and roar of the contending elements." [4]

The progressives wanted more effective
popular control, but they also wanted more
competent classroom performance; and like
Mann, they insisted that this required the development of a genuine profession of teaching. Moreover, since they deeply believed that

[4] George S. Counts, *School and Society in Chicago*
(New York: Harcourt, Brace & Co., 1928), pp. 353-54.
For the shift in the progressive position, compare
Counts's volume with Dr. J. M. Rice, *The Public-School
System of the United States* (New York: The Century
Co., 1893).

popular education demanded its own kind of teachers, thoroughly committed to the values of popular culture, they pressed for professional schools of education clearly differentiated from the more traditionally oriented academic institutions. Thus, to take one leading example, Dean James Earl Russell of Teachers College never ceased to point out that the College was the "professional school of Columbia University for the advanced professional training of teachers" and that its place in the university system was "analogous to that of the schools of Law, Medicine, and Applied Science." [5] As such, it assumed collegiate training as a prerequisite for entrance but considered "that the cultural discipline of the college course is no substitute for the technical equipment in the particular subject, which every teacher must acquire either by experience in the class-room or by professional training." [6]

There is a tension here, of course, that has been at the heart of the popular education sys-

[5] "An Appeal for Endowment, December 1, 1902," bound with Teachers College, Columbia University, *Report of the Dean, 1902.*

[6] Teachers College, Columbia University, *Report of the Dean, 1905,* p. 13.

tem from the very beginning. On the one hand, there is the prerogative of the public to set policy, determine direction, and fix support: we speak of public *control*, not merely public sponsorship or public influence. On the other hand, there is the prerogative of the teaching profession to govern its own work, set standards, and determine the nature of teaching practice: the teacher is committed to teaching truth as he sees it and to following truth wherever it leads.[7] Recognizing this tension, the late Charles Beard used to argue that a democratic society should support schools which must then be left free to criticize the society that supports them.[8] He had a point, though as we well know, the lower schools have rarely had genuine freedom to criticize regnant values in any searching way. What

[7] The tension is beautifully portrayed in Walter Lippmann's discussion of the trial of John T. Scopes at Dayton, Tennessee, and the trial of William McAndrew at Chicago, Illinois, in *American Inquisitors* (New York: The Macmillan Co., 1928).

[8] Beard made the point in a monograph he prepared for the Educational Policies Commission entitled *The Unique Function of Education in American Democracy* (Washington, D.C.: National Education Association, 1937), pp. 106-29. See also Alexander Meiklejohn, *Education Between Two Worlds* (New York: Harper & Brothers, 1942), pp. ix-x, 3-12.

little freedom they do have has been gained very slowly, and we have seen on occasion after occasion how precarious that freedom really is when basic commitments are at stake.[9]

In our own time, there have been proposals for strengthening both the public and the professional prerogatives. Several years ago, two books attracted a good deal of attention by advancing diametrically opposed recommendations. In *The Future of Public Education* (1960), Myron Lieberman pleaded for a

[9] In an early draft of a forthcoming book tentatively titled *Toward a Free Society*, Milton Konvitz points out that a number of recent United States Supreme Court decisions, notably, *Sweezy v. New Hampshire* (1957), have had the effect of giving academic freedom "full and equal First Amendment status" and that these decisions make no distinction between teachers in the public schools and university professors. Konvitz goes on to suggest that the Court has also provided a theoretical basis for student claims to academic freedom, viz., Justice Frankfurter's assertion in *Wieman v. Updegraff* (1952) that public opinion in a democracy must be "disciplined and responsible" and that it can only be disciplined and responsible if citizens, "in the formative years," acquire "habits of open-mindedness and of critical inquiry." The definition and scope of academic freedom were deeply involved, of course, in the political controversy at the University of California at Berkeley during the 1964-65 academic year. This particular aspect of the Berkeley controversy is best discussed by Elinor Langer in *Science*, CXLVIII (April 9 and 16, 1965), 198-202, 346-49.

much more powerful teaching profession, with authority to determine the scope, content, and character of schooling; only as schoolmen arrogated unto themselves all major decisions of educational policy would the crisis in education be solved. In *The Child, the Parent, and the State* (1959), on the other hand, James B. Conant contended that the battle for better schools would be won by the collective action of laymen in localities across the country. While Lieberman's argument proved the more attractive one in professional circles, Conant's is the more realistic, though it should be pointed out that in *Shaping Educational Policy* (1964), he has called for a massive strengthening of state departments of education and for the creation of an "Interstate Commission for Planning a Nationwide Educational Policy." Nevertheless, Conant's principal message has always been the same: only as a substantial and articulate public comes to prize first-rate popular education in this country will that commitment eventually be realized in practice.

2

There is, as Roald Campbell has suggested, a considerable folklore of local school control in the United States.[10] We are fond of pointing out that education is nowhere mentioned in the Constitution; that there are really fifty state systems of education and thirty thousand district systems; and that, in effect, public education remains the last stronghold of local citizen control. Now, there is great truth in these propositions. Each state does have broad powers to establish and maintain public schools; to regulate both public and private schools; to set certain minimum requirements for curricula, personnel, and buildings; to levy taxes for the support of education; to create and abolish school districts; and to establish and regulate their authority. And local districts do set tax rates, erect buildings, determine instructional policies, employ teachers and administrators, and generally oversee the day-by-day operation of the schools. The re-

[10] Roald F. Campbell, "The Folklore of Local School Control," *School Review*, LXVII (1959), 1-16.

sultant differences in support, control, and clientele color every aspect of American school life: programs of study, classroom teaching, out-of-class activities, discipline, and school-community relations. Whatever else may be said of American education, the cartoon of uniformity drawn by critics in the United States and abroad does not exist, and never has.

Yet one can grant all this and still talk about a folklore of local control, for the influences that have decisively shaped American education in our time have been not local but national in scope and character. Consider the pattern of formal influence. There is no denying that the years since World War II have witnessed a steady increase in Federal participation as Congress, acting under its mandate to "provide for the common Defence and general Welfare," has appropriated increasing sums of money for educational purposes. A study based on 1962 figures, for example, revealed that the Federal government was spending some $2.2 billion a year on education and research, of which about half was going directly to schools and colleges, and that this money was being disbursed by more than a dozen different Federal departments and agencies. Interestingly enough, the largest program that year was under the auspices not of the United States Office of Education but rather of the Department of Defense, which sponsored more educational activities and had a larger educational budget than all the other Federal departments combined.[11]

Some of this activity, to be sure, had little to do with the popular schools; but much of it affected them in exceedingly significant ways. The Office of Education was funneling millions of dollars into the support of vocational training, the preparation of guidance counselors, the development of language laboratories, and the retraining of classroom teachers. The National Science Foundation, through its Course Content Improvement Program, was subsidizing the redesign of elementary and secondary school science and social science programs throughout the country. And the Department of Defense was actually running the nation's ninth largest

[11] U.S., Congress, House, Committee on Education and Labor, *The Federal Government and Education*, 88th Congress, 1st Session, House Document No. 159 (Washington, D.C.: U.S. Government Printing Office, 1963).

school system—for the children of military personnel overseas.

We think initially about legislation, but actually the Federal agency that has shaped educational policy most powerfully since World War II has been not the Congress but the Supreme Court. Decisions such as *Everson* (1947), *McCollum* (1948), *Zorach* (1952), and especially *Brown* (1954) have dramatically altered the character of American education—the first three by slowly revising the relations between public and denominational education, and the last by substantially changing the organization of public education in the South and in the Northern cities.

Finally, I should add that we are witnessing in the progress of Lyndon B. Johnson's legislative program an unparalleled example of the power of the President to influence the nature and purposes of American popular education. Johnson himself has remarked that he would like to go down in history as the President who provided every American child with "all of the education, of the highest quality, which his or her ambition demands and his or her mind can absorb"; and he has more than demonstrated in his proposals to the Eighty-ninth Congress that this is no idle aspiration.[12]

One can properly dwell on these formal influences, but there are informal influences at least as significant. Professional organizations, regional accrediting associations, philanthropic foundations, the leading graduate faculties of education, textbook publishers, testing programs, committee reports, commission statements, analyses by influential individuals—all exercise a profoundly important nationalizing influence. The particular accreditation criteria of the North Central Association of Colleges and Secondary Schools, the particular programs financed by the Ford Foundation, the particular emphases of the College Entrance Examination Board's test in English, the particular approaches taught at Columbia or Harvard or Chicago or Stanford, the particular recommendations embodied in Conant's latest

[12] Address to the National Education Association, July 2, 1965, *New York Times,* July 3, 1965, p. 8. The efforts of the United States Office of Education to end racial segregation in the public schools are also an obvious example of executive influence. See *New York Times,* April 30, 1965, pp. 1, 21, and G. W. Foster, Jr., "Title VI: Southern Education Faces the Facts," *Saturday Review,* XLVIII (March 20, 1965), 60-1, 76-9.

report—all generate direct and specific changes in schools across the country.[13]

What I am really saying is that given a continuing localism, we have evolved what is in many respects a national system of education; and the fundamental political problem is not whether we shall have a measure of Federal control in education but how this control will be exercised and kept sufficiently responsive to the public. I am not suggesting that all national influences on education should be governmental. Nor am I insisting that every educational decision at the Federal level should be made by elected officials. I am simply urging that we frankly acknowledge that national policies in education are being worked out and that we devise ways of debating the leading issues and of opening the debate to public scrutiny. To quote from the now-classic formulation in John Dewey's *The Public and Its Problems:* "We have inherited . . . local town-meeting practices and ideas. But we live and act and have our being in a continental national state. We are

[13] See, for example, Roald F. Campbell and Robert A. Bunnell, eds., *Nationalizing Influences on Secondary Education* (Chicago: Midwest Administration Center, University of Chicago, 1963).

held together by non-political bonds, and the political forms are stretched and legal institutions patched in an *ad hoc* and improvised manner to do the work they have to do." [14]

In building the political forms to govern public education in what Dewey called "The Great Society," we need to keep several things in mind. First, there is all the difference in the world between centralized policy-making and centralized administration. The incredible bureaucratic inflexibility of our metropolitan school systems tells us what happens when we confuse the one with the other. My argument is that we need to develop appropriate methods for formulating and reviewing educational policy at the national level; but we need to be equally creative in devising ways of decentralizing the administration of those policies. [15] In

[14] John Dewey, *The Public and Its Problems* (New York: Henry Holt and Co., 1927), pp. 113-14.

[15] Interestingly enough, the progressives pressed for greater centralization of school control, holding that this would introduce greater efficiency and economy into school management and render the process of policy making more open to public scrutiny. Actually, in the matter of combining centralized control with decentralized administration, one can still learn much from the TVA experience, as reported by David E. Lilienthal in *TVA: Democracy on the March* (New York: Harper & Brothers, 1944).

the absence of such decentralization of administration, a certain priceless legacy of our public education system will be destroyed—its closeness and responsiveness to the public it serves.

Second, if we take seriously the rise of new forms of public education outside the schools, then we must ask what effective public control means with respect to the new media, for example, radio and television. Here, I would argue that the Federal Communications Commission is already in the business of making educational policy in the United States: it carries some of the classic responsibilities of a school board. And that being the case, it ought to employ genuine educational criteria in making some of its decisions. Since the right to a radio band or a television channel is a public franchise, the FCC ought to be much more stringent in its minimum public service requirements; and since radio and television are potentially of profound educational significance, the FCC ought to carry forward Frieda Hennock's admirable effort of the 1950's to reserve certain bands for educational purposes and then encourage their imaginative use. Moreover, Congress, which

broke new ground in 1962 by enacting legislation providing for the development of educational television, might well elaborate and expand that effort, viewing it as a major phase
of the Federal program in education.[16]

Finally, I should like to reiterate Beard's
dictum that a democratic society should support schools which must then be left free to
criticize the society that supports them. There
is an ever present danger in the popular control of popular education, which Tocqueville
called "the tyranny of the majority"—the insistence upon uniformity and acceptability of
ideas and ideals and the insistence upon service to society in its narrowest, most utilitarian sense. To the extent that such tyranny
prevails, popular education ceases to be education and becomes indoctrination in the com-
monest popular prejudices. Academic freedom
is the public's protection against such cheap-
ening; and it must be encouraged not merely
because it benefits scholars but because it benefits the society that sustains it. This, of course,
means tension, for given academic freedom

[16] Many of these issues are discussed forthrightly and
intelligently by Newton N. Minow in *Equal Time: The
Private Broadcaster and the Public Interest* (New York:
Atheneum, 1964).

no public relations effort on the part of educational administrators can obscure the conflict of ideas and ideals that will result. In the end, the democrat is sustained by the faith that such conflict is generally incident to the search for truth, beauty, and goodness. His opponents, who value order and uniformity above all things, will doubtless get more tranquil but less educative schools.

3

The progressives believed that universal education demanded a new profession of teaching, equipped by formal training to carry the arduous burdens of popular schooling. Moreover, they deeply believed that the development of a teaching profession required an independent faculty of education, with status in the university equal and analogous to that of the older faculties of medicine, law, and engineering. Such a faculty would deal with the "science and art of education" (though what that meant with respect to actual courses and programs was, from the beginning, a matter of controversy); and its strength would lie in its ability to control access to positions of leadership in the schools.[17]

Professional schools of education were duly established in universities across the country, and they grew rapidly in size, power, and influence; indeed, their rise is one of the leading educational developments of the twentieth century. But they have always been under attack from faculties of arts and sciences, and in recent years that attack has grown sharper. Actually, we have no scholarly assessment of their contribution in the large. It is easy enough to find trivia in their programs, and critics have enjoyed that sport to the fullest. But there is no denying that for all their shortcomings, they have managed to commit several generations of teachers to trying to teach all comers, often with inadequate resources, in overcrowded classrooms, and against overwhelming public indifference. As late as 1958,

[17] See Merle L. Borrowman, *The Liberal and Technical in Teacher Education* (New York: Bureau of Publications, Teachers College, Columbia University, 1956) and *Teacher Education in America: A Documentary History* (New York: Teachers College Press, Teachers College, Columbia University, 1965).

Harrison Salisbury found in a nationwide survey of delinquency that in slum neighborhood after slum neighborhood, the only adults who seemed to be engaged in really imaginative work with impoverished children were the schoolteachers.[18]

But whatever the accomplishments of education faculties, I am inclined to think that in the long run, the analogy to medicine, law, and engineering may have done more harm than good. This is not to deny that teaching is a profession, and it is not to deny that there should be professional schools of education. It is rather to argue that the faculty of education in any university maintains a unique relationship to the faculty of arts and sciences, and for good reasons. In the first place, the very nature of the teacher's job renders certain work given in the academic departments professional in character. For the aspiring teacher of history, courses with historians in the history department are as professional as they are liberal, and no amount of incantation about academicism can obscure that fact. Whether those courses should be taught in some special

[18] Harrison Salisbury, *The Shook-Up Generation* (New York: Harper & Brothers, 1958), pp. 157-58.

way for aspiring teachers is a moot point—I happen to think not, believing with Dewey that academic instruction in general would probably benefit if professors took seriously the fact that they were preparing some of their students to teach.[19] But whatever the answer to that question, there is no denying that arts and sciences professors are, by the very nature of their work and clientele, professionally involved in teacher education.

In the second place, if there was a case at the turn of the century for arguing that American colleges and universities were essentially elitist in orientation, and that the traditional arts and sciences faculties were not suited to prepare teachers committed to popular schooling, that case has long since lost its validity. The popularization of higher education since World War II, coupled with the development of new curricula that bring the most advanced research to the elementary school, has destroyed much of the disjunction that may have

[19] John Dewey, "The Relation of Theory to Practice in Education," in Charles A. McMurry, ed., *The Third Yearbook of the National Society for the Scientific Study of Education* (Chicago: University of Chicago Press, 1904), p. 24.

existed earlier. More than ever before, we have a ladder system of schooling in the United States, though there remains a healthy diversity in the character of schools at every level.

All this is merely to argue for a reunification of the teaching profession, for a healing of the breach that was created at the turn of the century between those who taught in the popular school system and those who taught in the colleges and universities.[20] It is to contend that the need is greater than ever for serious, sustained, scholarly inquiry into the ends and means of education, and to predict that this inquiry will be enhanced by the interest and participation of scholars in the arts and sciences. It is to argue, too, that faculties of arts and sciences need to give renewed attention to their role in the improvement of education at every level. I think the progressives were right when they insisted that no university could fulfill its responsibilities in the modern world without thinking seriously

[20] My argument here is similar to James B. Conant's in "A Truce Among Educators," *Teachers College Record*, XLVI (1944-45), 157-63.

about the popularization of knowledge. Nearly a century ago, Matthew Arnold, certainly no flaming pedagogical radical, stated it thus:

> The great men of culture are those who have had a passion for diffusing, for making prevail, for carrying from one end of society to another, the best knowledge, the best ideas of their time; who have laboured to divest knowledge of all that was harsh, uncouth, difficult, abstract, professional, exclusive; to humanise it, to make it efficient outside the clique of the cultivated and learned, yet still remaining the *best* knowledge and thought of the time, and a true source, therefore, of sweetness and light.[21]

Having spoken of the reunification of the teaching profession, I should like to argue also for the expansion of the profession to include what Martin Dworkin has called "the new educators." The proposal is hardly novel.

[21] Matthew Arnold, *Culture & Anarchy* (New York: The Macmillan Co., 1899), pp. 38-9. Incidentally, Dewey pointed to the relationship between his definition of culture and Arnold's in "Culture and Culture Values," in Paul Monroe, ed., *A Cyclopedia of Education* (5 vols.; New York: The Macmillan Co., 1911-13), I, 238-39.

Thirty-six years ago, shortly after coming to Teachers College, George S. Counts published an intriguing essay entitled "What Is a School of Education?" [22] In it, he chided his colleagues for conceiving of a school of education as an institution devoted "almost exclusively to the training of school teachers and to the study of the work of schools"; and he sketched an ideal school of education that embraced a College of Teachers, a College of Parenthood, a College of Religious Education, a College of Journalism, a College of Library Service, a College of Dramatics, a College of Exhibits and Excursions, a College of Recreation, a College of Adult Education, and, capping all of these, an Institute of Research and Synthesis.

His proposal was partly facetious, and yet it cut two ways: it implied that teachers had to develop a more realistic sense of the context of their work, and it suggested that there were many educational crafts that had yet to be professionalized. Now, I am not sure that Counts—or I, for that matter—would want to professionalize motherhood; but I do think

[22] George S. Counts, "What Is a School of Education?" *Teachers College Record*, XXX (1928-29), 647-55.

we should both like to see those who educate through agencies other than the school equipped with the same insights and understandings as those who staff the schools. Only then will they merit sufficient academic freedom—I use the term advisedly—to relieve them of the narrow obligation to further the values of whoever pays them; and only then will appropriate criteria be developed for judging the performance of the agencies they operate.

There is a final point to be made here. I have portrayed the relationship between the educational profession and the lay public as one of inherent strain and tension, in which the public possesses ultimate legal and financial authority. Given this relationship, it seems to me that the profession is obligated, both in its own interest and in the interest of the service it performs, to assist the public in developing an ever more sophisticated body of opinion about education. Two recent books that bear on the problem come immediately to mind: Neal Gross's fascinating analysis of the pressures to which school superintendents are constantly subjected and Richard Hofstadter's incisive history of anti-intellectualism in American life.[23] Each of these studies in its own way tells us how narrow and how limited public commitment to the schools has been in the absence of informed discussion concerning the ends and means of education.

In one respect, the teaching profession has only itself to blame. A political scientist friend of mine is fond of remarking that most people do not care about freedom of speech because they really have nothing to say. Similarly, too few educational leaders in the United States are genuinely preoccupied with educational issues because they have no clear ideas about education. And if we look at the way these leaders have been recruited and trained, there is little that would lead us to expect otherwise. They have too often been managers, facilitators, politicians in the narrowest sense. They have been concerned with building buildings, balancing budgets, and pacifying parents, but they have not been prepared to spark a great public dialogue about the ends and means of education. And in the absence of such a dialogue, large segments of the public have had,

[23] Neal Gross, *Who Runs Our Schools?* (New York: John Wiley & Sons, 1958) and Richard Hofstadter, *Anti-intellectualism in American Life* (New York: Alfred A. Knopf, 1963).

at best, a limited understanding of the whys and wherefores of popular schooling.

I think we need to train up a new kind of educational leader in this country if the great questions of educational purpose are to receive intelligent discussion by teachers and the lay public. This new kind of leader will obviously need fundamental preparation in the behavioral sciences to undergird his understanding of the nature of education and of the political processes by which educational policy is made. But beyond this, he will need fundamental preparation in the humanities of education, those studies of history, philosophy, and literature that will enable him to develop a clear and compelling vision of education and of its relation to American life.[24] These latter studies have been under something of a cloud in recent decades because their immediate utility is difficult to demonstrate. But it is their ultimate utility that really matters, for only as educators begin to think deeply about the ends of learning will the politics of popular education go beyond mere competition for

[24] The most relevant discussion I know is Robert Ulich, *Professional Education as a Humane Study* (New York: The Macmillan Co., 1956).

dollars and cents and become what Plato realized it must ideally be—a constant reaching for the good society.

4

As one reviews the American experience, nothing is more striking than the boundless faith of the citizenry in the power of popular education. It was a faith widely shared by the generation that founded the republic, and it has been an essential article of American belief ever since. Indeed, one literally cannot understand American history apart from it, so often have Americans expressed their political aspirations in educational terms. Education has been, par excellence, America's instrument of social progress and reform;[25] and it has com-

[25] The theme is developed in Rush Welter, *Popular Education and Democratic Thought in America*, though it should be added that whether education is actually a substitute for direct political action has always been a matter of debate. Thus, in the 1890's, critics of the social settlement referred to its essentially educational approach to the alleviation of poverty as "a fine Victorian example of rose water for the plague" (Jane

manded such widespread popular support that
D. W. Brogan was once moved to refer to the
public school as America's "formally unestab-
lished national church." [26]

Now, all this implies a measure of simple
optimism that has been anything but modish
in recent years. Faith in popular intelligence
has been sharply qualified of late, by Freudian
and Marxian attacks on rationality and by
elitist attacks on democracy. And notions of
infinite perfectibility seem hardly tenable in a
world that has used the fruits of science to
build gas chambers and hydrogen bombs. As
Henry David Aiken remarked not long ago
in a thoughtful reappraisal of the Deweyan
outlook, "Of course we, like Dewey, must
go on, hoping against hope that we may have
time and strength to learn how to control all
the creatures of Prometheus. But we no longer
have the fine old confidence of Dewey's
middle period that if we simply stick to the

Addams, *My Friend, Julia Lathrop* [New York: The
Macmillan Co., 1935], p. 57). And more recently, Chris-
topher Jencks leveled essentially the same criticism
against Lyndon B. Johnson's economic opportunity
program (*New Republic*, CL [March 28, 1964], 15-18).
[26] D. W. Brogan, *The American Character* (New
York: Alfred A. Knopf, 1944), p. 137.

method of science, or intelligence, all will be well and all manner of things will be well. I at least am just a little envious of Dewey in this regard. But my envy also marks the limits of his use to me." [27]

Are we left, then, only to envy the innocent confidence of a bygone age? I think not. I believe it is possible to espouse the optimism on which any program of popular education must rest without ending up either a utopian or a fool. With all its limitations, man's rationality remains his best instrument for comprehending and dealing with his experience; and as Harold Laski once said of democracy, in its absence men become the tools of others without available proof that the common good is involved.[28] What we must abandon, I think, is the age-old dream that education can ever usher in any sort of millennium. A century and a half ago, Jefferson wrote to his friend Du Pont de Nemours: "Enlighten the people generally, and tyranny

[27] *New York Review of Books*, IV (April 22, 1965), 18.
[28] Harold J. Laski, "Democracy," in Edwin R. A. Seligman and Alvin Johnson, eds., *Encyclopaedia of the Social Sciences* (15 vols.; New York: The Macmillan Co., 1930-35), V, 77.

and oppressions of body and mind will vanish like evil spirits at the dawn of day." [29] The sad reality, of course, is that tyranny and oppressions of body and mind will not vanish in our day any more than they did in Jefferson's. What we can continue to hope, it seems to me, is that men will learn to face their problems more intelligently in the future than they have in the past. And that would be progress indeed for humankind.

[29] Thomas Jefferson to Pierre Samuel du Pont de Nemours, April 24, 1816, in Dumas Malone, ed., *Correspondence between Thomas Jefferson and Pierre Samuel du Pont de Nemours, 1798-1817* (Boston: Houghton Mifflin Co., 1930), p. 186.

LAWRENCE A. CREMIN is Frederick A. P. Barnard Professor of Education and Director of the Institute of Philosophy and Politics of Education at Teachers College, Columbia University. A historian and social scientist as well as an educator, he brings to his subject a perspective and breadth of view unique in his profession. He has served as President of the History of Education Society and of the National Society of College Teachers of Education, and is currently Vice-President of the National Academy of Education. His articles and books are widely known, notably *The American Common School: An Historic Conception* (1951); *A History of Education in American Culture* (with R. Freeman Butts, 1953); and *The Transformation of the School: Progressivism in American Education, 1876-1957* (1961). The last-named was awarded the Bancroft Prize in American History for 1962.

THE TEXT of this book was set on the Linotype in Janson, an excellent example of the influential and sturdy Dutch types that prevailed in England prior to the development by William Caslon of his own designs, which he evolved from these Dutch faces. The book was composed, printed and bound by The Colonial Press Inc., Clinton, Massachusetts.

The Genius of American Education was first published by the University of Pittsburgh Press in its Horace Mann Lecture Series. It is available from the Press in a hardback edition.

Other titles in the Horace Mann Lecture Series published by the University of Pittsburgh Press are:

Francis S. Chase, *Education Faces New Demands*

George S. Counts, *Education and the Foundations of Human Freedom*

Allison Davis, *Psychology of the Child in the Middle Class*

Laurence D. Haskew, *The Discipline of Education and America's Future*

Francis Keppel, *Personnel Policies for Public Education*

Paul H. Masoner, *A Design for Teacher Education*

Ernest O. Melby, *The Education of Free Men*

Maurice J. Thomas, *Public Education and a Productive Society*

VINTAGE HISTORY—AMERICAN